Awaken:

Theory and Practice for the Aspiring Shaman

Composed by: Dr. Erik McBride, D.D., ULC Shaman

Table of Contents

Section 1: Philosophy and Theory of the Shaman

1. Into Existence *page 10*
2. The Seven Planes *page 12*
3. Spiritual Energy *page 16*
4. Spirit and Soul *page 19*
5. Materialized and Imagined Manifestations *page 21*
6. The Cycle of Life and Death *page 23*
   A. The Material Manifestation *page 23*
   B. Moral Issues of the Cycle *page 24*
7. Path of the Shaman *page 27*
8. Meditation and Awareness *page 29*
   A. Deep Tissue Relaxation *page 29*
   B. Following the Breath *page 31*
9. Awakening *page 34*
10. For Contemplation *page 36*

Section 2: Preparation for Magic

1. Introduction *page 38*
2. Categories of Magic *page 41*
3. Tools of the Shaman *page 44*
4. The Magic Circle *page 50*

       A. Magic Sand *page 52*

5. The Aura *page 54*

       A. Aura of Spirit *page 54*

       B. Emotional Energy Centers *page 55*

       C. Etheric Aura *page 56*

       D. Life Fire Aura *page 59*

       E. Five Gates Breath Exercise *page 61*

       F. Auric Tendrils *page 63*

       G. Earth and Cosmic Auras *page 65*

       H. Circulating the Etheric Aura *page 68*

       I. Personal Vortex *page 70*

6. Differing Magic Spells from Magic Ritual *page 73*

       A. The Magic Spell *page 73*

       B. The Magic Ritual *page 74*

       C. Keep Your Own Counsel *page 76*

7. Transcendence from Material Consciousness *page 77*

8. Holy Days of the Shaman *page 80*

    A. Vernal Equinox *page 80*

    B. Summer Solstice *page 81*

    C. Autumnal Equinox *page 81*

    D. Winter Solstice *page 82*

    E. Full Moon *page 82*

    F. New Moon *page 82*

    G. Other Events *page 83*

9. Minerals and Magic *page 84*

10. Raising Energy for Effects *page 85*

Section 3: The Sacred Teacher Plants

1. All Things Being Sacred *page 88*

2. Shamans and the Sacred Teacher Plants *page 89*

3. Communion *page 91*

4. Vision Quest *page 94*

5. Consulting the Oracle *page 96*

6. Magical Empowerment *page 98*

7. Cultivation and Preparation *page 100*

    A. Argyria Nervosa "Baby Hawaiian Wood Rose" *page 101*

    B. Banisteriopsis Caapi "Ayahuasca Vine" *page 103*

    C. Cannabis Sativa "Indian Hemp" *page 106*

    D. Desmanthus Illinoensis "Prairie Mimosa" *page 109*

      E. Ephedra Major "Ma Huang" *page 112*

      F. Erythroxylum Coca "Coca Bush" *page 114*

      G. Ipomoea Violacea "Tri-Color Morning Glory" *page 117*

      H. Lophophora Williamsii "Peyote" *page 119*

      I. Nicotiana Rustica "Turkish Tobacco" *page 122*

      J. Papaver Somniferum "Opium Poppy" *page 124*

      K. Peganum Harmala "Syrian Rue" *page 126*

      L. Phalaris Arundinacae "Gardener's Garters" *page 128*

      M. Psilocybe Cubensis "Magic Mushrooms" *page 130*

      N. Psychotria Viridis "Chacruna" *page 135*

      O. Salvia Divinorum "Diviner's Sage" *page 138*

      P. Tabernanthe Iboga "Iboga Root" *page 140*

      Q. Trichocereus Pachanoi "San Pedro" *page 143*

8. Proper use of the Sacred Teacher Plants *page 146*

Section 4: Magic Manual

1. Introduction *page 148*

2. Conjuring Images *page 149*

      A. Exercise 1: Forming a Globe *page 150*

      B. Exercise 2: Conjuring a Butterfly *page 151*

      C. Exercise 3: The Cloak of Shadows *page 153*

      D. Exercise 4: Changing the Façade *page 154*

      E. Exercise 4 Part A: Masking the Eyes *page 155*

- F. Exercise 4 Part B: Masking the Facial Structure *page 156*
- G. Exercise 4 Part C: Masking the Body Structure *page 158*
- H. Spectres, Doppelgangers, and Lycanthropy *page 159*
- I. Exercise 5: Forming the Spectre *page 160*
- J. Exercise 6: Forming the Doppelganger *page 161*
- K. Exercise 7: Conjuring the Form of the Lycanthrope *page 163*

3. Elemental Magic *page 166*
   - A. The Elemental State *page 166*
   - B. Exercise 1: Changing the Elemental State *page 167*
   - C. Manipulating Energies of the Material Plane *page 169*
   - D. Exercise 2: Influencing the Candle Flame *page 169*
   - E. Exercise 3: Influencing the Pendulum *page 171*
   - F. Exercise 4: Binding the Light *page 172*

4. Emotional Empathic Magic *page 175*
   - A. The Suggestive Presence *page 175*
   - B. Exercise 1: The Presence of Lust *page 176*
   - C. Exercise 2: The Presence of Terror *page 178*
   - D. Emotional Wyrms *page 179*
   - E. Exercise 3: Forming the Wyrm *page 180*
   - F. Exercise 4: Removing a Wyrm *page 181*

5. Enchantment *page 184*
   - A. Exercise 1: Prayer Beads for Peace *page 185*
   - B. Exercise 2: The Amulet of Benevolence *page 186*

- C. Exercise 3: The Rune of Warding *page 188*
- D. Exercise 4: The Seal of Protection *page 190*
- E. Exercise 5: Forming the Doll *page 192*
- F. Exercise 6: Shaping a Fetch *page 193*

6. Life Magic *page 195*
    - A. Exercise 1: Aiding in a Swift Recovery *page 195*
    - B. Exercise 2: Banishing Parasites *page 197*
    - C. Exercise 3: Changing Flesh to Iron *page 198*
    - D. Exercise 4: Charging the Marrow *page 200*
    - E. Necromancy *page 202*
    - F. Exercise 5: Ghouls *page 203*
    - G. Exercise 6: Resurrection *page 204*

7. The Perceptive Arts *page 206*
    - A. Divination *page 206*
    - B. Tarot *page 207*
    - C. Scrying *page 214*
    - D. Clairvoyance *page 216*

8. Spiritism *page 217*
    - A. Exercise 1: Plant Telepathy *page 217*
    - B. Exercise 2: Animal Telepathy *page 219*
    - C. Exercise 3: Mediumship *page 220*
    - D. Exercise 4: Channeling *page 221*

9. Limitless Possibilities *page 223*

Bibliography *page 225*

Web Resources *page 229*

Index *page 230*

Section 1:

Philosophy and Theory of the Shaman

Into Existence

Ultimately, we are non-existence. We are not nothing; we do exist, but the thing from which all existence itself came cannot be described or properly labeled in a way of which we are now capable. This is especially true considering the very limited linear form of communication we bind ourselves to on the Material Plane. We came from the Ultimate, the non-thing, and to it we return in our time.

With two opposing motions, a pushing and a pulling which worked upon each other, awareness was born. With awareness, the motion became; without awareness, no existence could be possible for there would be no knowledge of this existence. The motion existed, and it was aware of its existence.

From the first swirling of the Original Motion, vibrations grew. These are not of the physical, material type; these are purely spiritual and only with the awareness of the Spirit can they be known. These vibrations are of three in type: Light, Sound, and Touch. Awareness swelled with the Three Vibrations, and this awareness developed an understanding for the way the Original Motion had turned to form it. By understanding of the way it had turned, understanding of the way it will turn and is turning was found. This growth of awareness is the Universal Consciousness, and the way all energies will twist, have twisted, and are twisting are understood by it and will be so until the end of existence itself.

The Universal Consciousness was aware of different patterns of the Three Vibrations; this awareness spread into the different patterns, and they became aware of their differences. Thus was the birth of the Individual, and the Spirit itself. These

Individual Spirits retained the knowledge and understanding of the Universal Consciousness, for they are not separate from it and this also is understood.

Simple awareness within the patterns that formed the Individual Spirits grew into a consciousness, with an understanding of how to release new vibrations from within. These new vibrations are called Emotions, and the Emotional Vibrations shook the Individual Spirits and drowned out the voice of understanding from the Universal Consciousness. The light of the Emotions led the Spirits to understand intentions and desires, and to learn the ways of directing the Three Vibrations to form Manifestations. The Spirits also learned how to share their Emotional Vibrations with others, striking chords of harmony and discord amongst one another.

Desires and intentions coupled with the knowledge of how to form Manifestations and churn the Three Vibrations themselves moved the Spirits into conflict with one another. No part of a Spirit can be changed save for the Emotional Vibrations, and with them the desire and intentions of that Spirit. This turned the conflict to that of command over the Manifestations and Nature of the Manifestations. The conflict formed three distinctions: the locking of Will, in which Nature was determined; a place where Imagination, the failure to gain dominance reigned; and the Material, where command of the Manifestations and Nature of the Manifestations came into existence.

With the formation of Reality and dominance over the Nature of the Manifestations and the Manifestations determined, the Spirits were free to watch over their place of Materials, but not free to experience it as though they were the Manifestations themselves. Many different combinations of the Manifestations according to their established Natures were formed, and through these differences combining, a new vibrational energy was found, this one purely Material. This energy was called Life Fire, for it had the ability to give awareness to the Material by way of containing the essence of an Individual Spirit itself.

The Cycle of Life and Death began with this, for a Spirit cannot retain its awareness within the Material without the Life Fire being constantly replenished. Life Fire can be replenished of itself, as it was originally formed; however, many Spirits had forgotten all but the Material they had become. Thus, the devouring of other Manifestations of Spirit became a necessity for the forgetful to retain their existence upon the Material Plane.

Many who had come to the Material Plane had forgotten those things they had set out to experience before journeying here. Emotions and the Primal Desires of hunger for food, hunger for sex, and hunger for comfort reigned in the Material Consciousness of the Manifestations. Wars began for these three, and the idea of possession was birthed. Despite the loss of awareness and the blinding nature of the Material Consciousness, some of the Spirits were able to awaken within their Manifestations. These Enlightened Ones were called by many names across many lands, but their purpose was the same for all: Awaken the sleeping Spirits of the Manifestations!

The Seven Planes

Seven distinctive Planes form the total of existence. Each of these Planes is formed by its predecessor, and is superimposed upon it. In this way, all Seven Planes unite to form one.

The Plane of Motion is the 1st Plane. This consciousness, or mental state, of this plane is that of simple awareness of motion. The motion is aware that it is motion, but it is not aware of its awareness on this level. Push and Pull tug to form this Plane, winding the circle represented best by the Yin-Yang symbol from the Oriental cultures. The Plane of Motion is the origin of all that is, the original splitting of the Ultimate into opposition.

The Plane of the Universal Consciousness follows the 1st Plane. The substance of this Plane is like a cloudy mass of the Spirit Vibrations of Light, Sound, and Touch. Awareness of the Original Motion has grown into understanding of the motion and of the awareness, thus forming a consciousness. This Universal Consciousness expands beyond change and what we consider to be time; all motions that will be can be seen by what has been, and that is the understanding of the Universal Consciousness. The unified state of being of this Plane is often called the Great Spirit, for it is from this Spirit that the fabric and awareness of all others stem.

The Plane of Individuality sees the birth of many different patterns of the Three Vibrations forming from the Great Spirit. On this 3rd Plane, the awareness of distinction is found within the patterns, and Individual Spirits become. These Spirits are lacking of volition, but are full of understanding of their own origins, structure, and that of all other individuals.

The 4th Plane is the Plane of Emotion. It is here that the awareness of individuality expands into a consciousness and an understanding of how to churn the Three Vibrations from within. These new Vibrations of Spirit are termed Emotional Energies, and spread from one Spirit to the next by means of harmonious or discordant resonance. This resonance leads to the impression of changes by one Spirit upon the next, and in accord, desires and intentions from desires arise. It is by desire that the first of the Manifestations, the Elementals, are formed from the Three Vibrations by use of the Emotional Energies. Because not all Spirits resonate emotions in harmony, a battle for command of the Three Vibrations and the formation of the Manifestations ensued, forming the next three Planes.

The Plane of Imagination is the 5th Plane, the land of dreams and mental wanderings. Desires strong enough to push energies, but not strong enough to win the combat for command over them Manifest herein; all dreams and ideas first form here. The landscape of this Plane is fleeting, and can be manipulated with little Will applied.

The Plane of Reality, also known as The Shroud, composes the 6th of the Planes. This is the battleground for command of Manifestations and their Natures. It is formed of locked energies, with a solid command line for a consciousness. The nature of its consciousness is generally, "This may be, and this may not be." It is from this Plane that the Nature of the 7th is determined; changing its line of what may and may not be will change the composition of the 7th Plane.

The 7th Plane is the Material Plane. It is upon this Plane that Spirits bind themselves with Life Fire in effort to gain greater understandings. This Plane was created by the tug of war by all Spirits, and its Nature may change only by turning the tide of the battle itself. The Cycle of Life and Death rules this Plane for one who is within it; for one who is without, desire to experience the Plane from within motivates them to find a Manifestation which can bind them with the Life Fire. Most Magic performed is directed at this Plane, or directed to change this Plane in some way.

Spiritual Energy

In essence, there are only two types of Spiritual Energy. This is the duality of the Original Motion; an energy that gathers and an energy that disperses. One is a gravity, pulling other energies to itself, and the other is a radiation that pushes all other energies away from itself. These two energies dance with one another in spirals, and the different spirals become the Three Vibrations.

The Three Vibrations are formed by the three types of spiral the Original Motion makes. One appears as Light, and the other as Sound, and the last as Touch, or pressure. These Vibrations are not the same as Material qualities with which they share names.

Spiritual Light is a spiral of dominance by the radiation aspect of the Original Motion. It spreads outward, and bounces away from all things it comes into contact with. In this way, it is like Light, for it spreads out, illuminating the façade of all things by the way it moves away from them.

Spiritual Sound is an equality of the gravitating and radiating aspects of the Original Motion. The two force will not touch, or fly apart for that matter. The strain of one to pull in the other, and the other to repel the one creates a song. For this reason, it is termed Spiritual Sound.

Spiritual Touch or pressure is a complete dominance of the gravitating aspect of the Original Motion. It draws in upon itself all others around it which can be grasped. It is the complete opposite of Spiritual Light, and the two balance one another. The sensation of the grasp of this spiral is very much a pressure, and so it is termed Spiritual Touch.

These Three Vibrations combine with one another in seven distinct patterns, called the Emotional Energies. These are Compassion, Elation, Fear, the Love-Hate duality, Courage, Depression, and Malice. From these seven, nearly an infinite number of more complex emotions may be drawn, but these are the most basic form there is. Three spirals of the Three Vibrations form each of these Emotions.

Emotional Energies felt while within a Material Manifestation will undoubtedly affect its state of being. Emotions are not, however, physical sensations. They are purely Spiritual, very subtle, and intangible of themselves. Their effects upon the body are quite tangible, and can be disastrous or most beneficial to it. For this reason, the Emotional Energies and the way you personally respond to them should be contemplated in depth. Understanding them for what they are, combinations of vibrations, rather than the results they stir within you will lead you to a much greater understanding of all things.

From the desires of the Emotional Energies was Life Fire formed. Life Fire is a spectacular energy, capable of binding the awareness that is a Spirit into an animated Material Manifestation. Without it, Spirits would only play at constructing and destructing Manifestations; with it, they can become the Manifestation itself, and forget who they were.

There are many energies of the Material Plane: kinesis, heat, electro-magnetics, radio frequencies, light, and possibly countless others of which we are not yet aware. The Original Motion, the Three Vibrations, Emotional Energies, and Life Fire are not tangible like those of the Material, however. Material Energies can be measured and recorded with instruments of the Material Plane, but Spiritual Energies will more likely than not never be touched by those physical instruments. Only by increasing your awareness will be able to understand these energies better, and thus see the energies themselves rather than just the effects of the energies.

Spirit and Soul

      Individuality is formed not only by our distinctive patterns, but by our awareness and consciousness. The awareness and consciousness of a person is their Spirit. In the Material, the Spirit is the aspect of your personality that always watches you, that is a part of you, but seems to be disconnected from you. The Spirit records the way you experience things, as well as what you experience. You will notice that you do not always experience things for what they are, when you watch with the immoveable perception of your Spirit and compare it with the way the torrential downpour of Emotions will sway you to experience the same item. For instance, a person bumps into you, and you spill your drink all over yourself. How do you react to it? Are you reacting purely to the bump and the spill itself, or to the Emotions you generate because of the mishap? Contemplate this. When you are able to react to simply the spill itself, with no Emotional sway whatsoever, you will understand your Spirit.

      The Soul is the body of Emotional Energies of the Spirit. This body is desire itself. From this body, your Will and Volition assert themselves upon existence by generation of the Emotional Energies. Many are not aware of the way their Emotional Energies tug at the currents of existence, or even that they do. There are those who regard Emotions as simply physical states, chemical reactions in the body due to environment stresses. The Soul does cause change within the Material Manifestation, but the change is not the Emotion itself, it is a reaction to the Emotion. The Emotion itself is a spiral of pushes and pulls seeking to force the currents of existence into a different direction. This is desire, this is the Soul, and those who are not aware fear the Soulless because those who are free from the sway of desire are capable of generating it at will, and remaining untouched by the Emotions of others. Becoming desire-less is not enlightenment; understanding the Emotions and existence for what it is, even when you cannot put it into words, is Enlightenment.

Materialized and Imagined Manifestations

The Plane of Imagination and the Material Plane are very closely related. Each one is just as "real" as the other, though the Material Plane will very much attract a greater degree of attention (narrowing of awareness) than the Imagination will. Both are formed by Emotional Energies, though the Plane of Imagination is composed by a great a deal of a lesser amount of energy flow than the Material Plane. This means that the Plane of Imagination is shaped more readily by desire than the Material Plane, making it a suitable place to practice for what one will encounter in the Material Plane. Care should be taken not to confuse the two, however; this confusion can blind one's awareness so badly that it is nearly impossible to separate the being of one from the other.

Manifestations of the Material Plane are subject to Reality, the Will of the Shroud. This Will is the ultimate flow of all currents and the desires set upon them, and it is quite difficult to summon enough Emotion to change the Nature of the Shroud and therefore, the Nature of the Material Plane or the Plane of Imagination, even. Material Manifestations are subject to an extreme rigidity of actions and processes, and there is no other way but to flow as directed by these things.

The Plane of Imagination is also subject to the Will of the Shroud, and has its own Nature. It is more pliable than the Material, so Manifestations may be summoned up, destroyed, changed, or even assumed with very little desire. Spirits who are not bound to the Material Plane may manifest here with ease in whatever form is desired. This Plane is as real as the Material Plane, but they simply cannot interact with each other. The

Shroud is like a wall that blocks the Manifestations of the one from reaching to the Manifestations of the other, and regulates the both of them.

The Cycle of Life and Death

Like a wheel ever turning is the Cycle. Life Fire binds the Spirit to the Form, and Desire generates the Form and the leading of the Spirit to it. Death is the end of the Spirit's binding to a particular form, and its exit from the Material Plane.

Spirits join the Cycle through desire. The pull of Emotions lead a Spirit to be bound to a Manifestation in order to experience certain things and gain certain understandings. Thus, a Soul comes to inhabit a body. Unfortunately, the entry into the Cycle is so Emotionally traumatic that the Soul cannot remember its reasons for entering the Cycle, and the awareness of the Spirit is buried in the currents of Emotion.

The Material Manifestation

The Consciousness of the Manifestation is the foreground of awareness for an individual in the Cycle. This consciousness calls out for three things: sustenance, sex, and comfort. These three are the only things the body itself needs to survive. All other perceived "needs" are little more than combinations of desire and Manifestations of the Plane of Imagination. The Material Consciousness is also only capable of experiencing certain sensations in itself, and all are Material. These sensations are: pain, as a result of injury to the body; tension and relaxation of tissues; sexual tension and release; physical panic, resulting in fight, flight, or freeze; physical depression, as in lethargy of the limbs; tiredness of sleep and exhaustion; tickle and itch; pangs of need for nourishment; fidgety or restlessness of the tissues; and comfortable. Of course there are combinations of these feelings, or degrees, but these are the most basic feelings. The Material Manifestation itself cannot be happy, sad, or excited, but it can show the effects from these Emotions. Contemplate this to develop awareness of the difference between physical sensations and Emotional states.

Moral Issues of the Cycle

Moral conduct is a large issue for humans within the Cycle. Most of these are based on cultural pretenses and dogma passed on from parents to children for many generations, and some are based on prejudices steeped in intentional states of ignorance. All moral issues stem from the Emotions, and the trained responses of the Emotions in relation to these issues. Each must judge for him or herself what is moral and what is not, rather than following the dictations of others without questioning, for an action is merely an action, containing and releasing only the Emotions we place within it. There is no good and there is no evil, except what we term as such and react to it as if it were what we termed it. The thing itself cannot be one or the other, only the way in which we view it is as such. Still, some are unsure where to begin, so we will establish a few basics of structure.

Killing is absolutely necessary if you wish to continue to live. For one to eat and survive, another must perish and be devoured. Slogans such as "meat is murder" try to steer people away from devouring the flesh of animals, so they can find Emotional absolution in the fact that nothing cute and cuddly is sizzling in their frying pan. That slogan and others like it can be misleading, for eating corn, broccoli, or even a pear is just as much murder as eating a cow or the stray cat that comes to your door. You must kill to live, regardless of what or whom you are eating. There are also issues of killing to protect one's own life or the life of their offspring or family. This is also a part of the Cycle, and in it there is no good and no evil. You must kill to eat, and you may have to kill to protect the lives of those to whom you have devoted yourself. If it is so, then so be it, and place no Emotions in it.

Sex is another moral issue. This is a natural process of creating offspring, and no wrong can be found in it. However, if the sex desired will harm another individual, it's best not to have it. Anything that will harm another individual, aside from protecting self and kin, and eating, is best left not done. Chances are that your harmful intentions are from out-of-control Emotions coupled with Images of what you wish to occur. Be aware when you wish to harm of why you want to do so.

Obligation to offspring and those you pledge to care for is the last moral issue we will discuss here. When you have children, you have sworn to care for them to the best of your ability even if it kills you. Regardless of whether you feel you want the child or not, this is how it should be handled. Whether you remember it or not, you managed a deal with your children from the Spirit to enable them to experience certain things. Treat them as they should be treated. As for those whom you pledge service to, such as a mate, a ward, or even a pet, care for them in the same manner you would treat your children. Be prepared to lie down your life for them, or do not take them into your care.

That which is was meant to be, or it could not be. Take things for as they are, not how you "feel" about them. Emotions will distract your awareness, and you will not be able to experience things as they are. Do not try to block them out, especially with moral issues. Utilize your Emotional Energies, especially with moral issues, and draw an understanding of yourself for why you react the way you do to certain occurrences, and differently for others. Practice acceptance, for what is must be, but do not fail to try to change existence in the way you wish it to be…once you understand what it is that you actually wish for.

Path of the Shaman

A Shaman is an individual within the Cycle who strives to both awaken the awareness of all sleeping Spirits and to change the Material Plane by directed desire. For this to be, the Shaman must personally be aware and of a still center in regards to the voracious winds of Emotions. Only by stilling the Emotions can one become aware, and only through awareness can one work Magic by Will (Will is the conscious direction of Emotional Energies, also known as desire, combined with Intention, which is precise construction of Imaginings.)

Any being existent upon the Material Plane can be a Shaman. Animals, plants, and people are all Spirits, and are all bound within the same currents of Emotion as is the rest of this Plane. Becoming a Shaman is a possibility for anyone with the determination and patience to work with their consciousness in order to garner awareness.

A Shaman seeks to expand his or her knowledge not only in the quest of self, but also in the more mundane arts. Being well-rounded in the sciences is of great benefit in both working magic and helping to awaken the sleepers. It is highly encouraged to study herbal medicine, first aid, farming techniques, technologies, history, and languages. The more you know, the more effective you will become in working with others to help them gain awareness. You will find that just being aware in itself seems to encourage others to wake up on their own better than any type of preaching or beating will do. Learn as much as possible, and utilize the skills you develop!

Magic is the art the Shaman uses to cause changes in the consciousness of others and changes to the Material Plane. These effects of Magic are not performed by physical or Material means, but by Spiritual means. Will is the way of the Shaman in regards to Magic; however, when a Shaman is presented with a choice of employing Magic or a Material means, the wise one will choose the most simple of the two.

Meditation and Awareness

Meditation is the process of gathering awareness. Most of the time, our awareness is scattered and fleeting; it leaps from one point of interest to another so swiftly that we in many instances do not even really notice where our awareness is settled. Though meditation, we are able to tame the random bounding of our awareness and settle it upon what we choose for it to be settled upon. We can only understand that of which we are aware; by practicing steadfast awareness, we are able to gain more understanding of ourselves, others, and the world around us.

Deep Tissue Relaxation

Though it is not entirely necessary for the body to be as relaxed as possible during meditation, this state is very helpful to the process. This is especially true during the earlier stages of meditation, when it is more difficult to just sit still and observe. The most supportive state of consciousness for becoming aware of the origins of our Emotions is the place just between sleeping and waking. When the body is restless, it can be very difficult to allow your mind to settle and your thoughts to still. Deep Tissue Relaxation is a technique by which the body can be placed in a state of extreme comfort.

Begin by seating yourself in a comfortable position with your entire body well supported. Reclining without lying completely prone is a good position to start with, for you will be sitting up just enough to stay awake and still lying back enough to allow the entire body to be supported. Once you are settled into your seat, take a deep, slow breath through your nostrils. Stop inhaling before your lungs are completely full, and exhale slowly through your mouth. As you exhale, feel your body sink into the chair as your tension flows outward with your breath. Inhale again through your nose, more slowly than with the first breath, and stop again before your lungs reach complete fullness. Relax your chest and abdomen, allowing the air to settle down deep into your diaphragm, then exhale. It is important to relax the area of your ribs and stomach; many of us tend to hold these tightly during our day-to-day activities for fear of others viewing us as fat. Holding this tense restricts your ability to breathe in the quantity of air you need per breath, so relax this area as much as possible as you exhale. Now, breathe in again through the nose, slowly allowing the air to fill your lungs, and just swiftly enough to feel comfortable. Allow the tensions of your entire body to drain into your lungs, and exhale deeply, sighing with pleasure as your body drains away its discomforts.

Now inhale again, and place your awareness upon your toes, feet, and ankles. When the point of inhalation ends, tense these as hard as you can until you feel the need to exhale. When you exhale, release your toes, feet, and ankles, allowing them to rest limp where they are. With the next breath, you will tense your calves and shins as hard as you can hold them after inhaling. With the exhale, release your hold on them immediately, allowing the tension to flow outwards with the air. The thighs and butt will follow the calves and shins. Upon the peak of your inhale, you will tense them as tightly as you can, and you will then release them as you exhale. After the thighs and butt, the stomach and lower back will follow. Tense these after the inhale, and release them on the exhale. The following breath will bring you to the chest and upper back. Tighten them with the completion of your inhale, and then relax them upon your exhale. Now you will tighten your fingers, hands, and wrists as much as you possibly can, after you inhale once again. Release the tension and exhale. Follow this with another inhale, and tense the forearms. Exhale and relax the forearms, then inhale and tense your upper arms and shoulders. Now relax your upper arms and shoulders, and exhale. Inhale again, and you will tighten your neck, throat, and the back of your head, holding them until you exhale. Now inhale again, and tighten your face, forehead, and the top of your head. Relax and exhale. Inhale deeply again, but this time, tighten your entire body at once as much as you are capable of. Relax when you exhale. At this point, your body will feel so relaxed and supple that it is very difficult to tense your muscle. Even so, inhale and tense it again. Relax with your exhale, and for the last time, inhale and tense, relax and exhale. With this last squeeze of your body, you have completed the process and are free to meditate, or simply bask in the comfort of total freedom from tension.

Following the Breath

Placing your awareness upon your entire environment at once without focusing on one or just a very few details can be excessively difficult. When practicing this, it is not necessary to attempt to shut out your thoughts (Imaginings and Emotions brought about by one another;) instead, just keep your attention upon both your body and the sensations you are experiencing through your body. Notice the sounds that strike your eardrums, the feeling of the air upon your skin, any scents that reach your nostrils, and tension in your muscles. Feel the pattern of your heartbeat and the blood rushing through your veins, and see whatever it is that lies before you without focusing your eyes on any one spot or moving them about all over the place. Accept all the perceptions at once for exactly as they are without placing any Emotions into them, or focusing your attention upon any single perception. When your thoughts drag you away, do not fight them off, but return to the pattern of your breath, and if you must, count them from one to ten.

This exercise can be tiring and boring at first, so start by practicing for just a few minutes two or three times a day. As you continue, you will find your thoughts begin to settle and your awareness expand, and the sessions can be extended to ten minutes or more. Years of practice may find you meditating upon your environment for hours at a time because of the peacefulness it brings within the Emotional storm. Be certain to practice daily when you first start, and even more so when you are years into it. Just a few moments a day are all that is necessary to reap the many benefits from following your breath.

When distracting thoughts arise during meditation, which they most certainly will, do not attempt to stop thinking them. This will generate more of your awareness upon the distractive thought and negate your general purpose. Instead, recognize the thought for being simply what it is. For instance, if you have a thought about a car, note it with "having a thought about a car," and return to your breathing, and counting of it if you do so. Place no Emotion within the fact that a thought has interrupted you or even the thought itself. Simply note its presence and allow it to pass. After a time of sitting in this way, you will notice many recurring thoughts and patterns of them. This is necessary in garnering awareness, and the long-term goal of following the breath: understanding the self.

The entire purpose of existing in the Cycle is to gain understanding. The different understandings we have laid out for ourselves to learn can only be learned when we are aware. This awareness must be of our environment as it is, the way we react to things with Emotion, and why we make the choices we make. Through meditation, we are able to reach a deeper level of awareness of these things, and thus we are able to achieve a greater understanding. The keys to your self are waiting for you to see them in your hand; open your eyes and look!

Meditation is not the end exercise or process in awareness and understanding. It is the beginning of perception, for only by it are we able to clear away the smoke screen of Emotions and Imaginings. Practice it diligently so that you will be able to direct the gaze of your Third Eye intentionally and precisely. Without dexterous view of the Third Eye as developed through Following the Breath and other techniques, the Sacred Plants will not be able to help your perception, only cloud it further.

Awakening

Awakening is the goal that cannot be grasped without first understanding why we slumber. To do this, "I" must become no more than a reference point. The illusion of internal and external must be overcome for you to end your slumber; this is illusion is the prison and the sleep. Shamanism is a path by which you can seek to awaken. Shamanism is not the only path and the final answer for all, just as the imprisoning concept of "I" is not the same for all. Seek the path and the way that is most befitting to yourself, and you will overcome. Seek power and glory, and you will tighten your shackles and secure your prison.

Actions of sanity only include those things benefiting your material existence. These sane actions are carnal: the quest for nourishment, for comfort, and for sex. Carnality, or sanity, is not inherently bad or evil. These are necessary for the continuance of physical existence and must be provided to an extent if you wish to survive. The Path of the Shaman is not a quest for these carnal things. This Path is the way of insanity and holiness, for only those things which seek to unite all as one in understanding are holy. Carnal actions cannot be holy, for they are selfish and again, neither bad nor evil by nature. Shamanism and Spirituality are not for the sane or for those who seek a grandiose existence in this lifetime. If you seek understanding, full awareness, and an experiential existence of the holy, or the One, you walk a path of insane actions for these actions cannot benefit your flesh. Sleeping is not evil just as Awakening is not good; however, the call is out to you now to make your choice of which you will have. Take responsibility for your decision and seek the end you have determined to its fullest potential.

For Contemplation

True Love is unconditional acceptance of all things as they are, completely unbiased by the perception of "within" and "without."

Awareness enters the Material Manifestation from without, from the unified point. This awareness is often blocked by the perceptions of the Material Manifestation, and ideas we have already formed of these perceptions. The key to absolving within and without lies with the ability for the Manifestation to perceive the origins of consciousness itself.

The body is a transceiver for consciousness. The "I" exists between the reception and the transmission; this consciousness itself, the observer part of the mind, is the Individual Spirit.

Section 2:

Preparation for Magic

Introduction

You will find the information contained in this section most helpful when you begin to form your own effects of Magic. An explanation of Magic itself and how it is performed, tools used and why they are used, and some other essential basics will be presented to you before proceeding into the actual Magic practices. Without a clear understanding of what actually makes Magic possible, it can be difficult to perform even the slightest of effects; this section should provide you with the basic understandings required to develop a mastery over at least one of the many branches of Magical workings.

We will define magic as: **motivating energies by direct action of Will to effect change.** This includes gathering knowledge through means such as Clairvoyance or Scrying. When you utilize Magic, you are directly shaping existence itself by means of your Emotions, which pull, push, or steady the flow of the currents of energy that compose all that is.

Performing Magic requires Will and Awareness. Will is a combination of clear vision of what you wish performed, known as intention, as well as a strong source of Emotional energies with which to form your intentions, known as desire. Will stems from the Soul, the body of an individual that is pure Emotion. To develop strong Will, you must learn to visualize, or form the Plane of Imagination, with perfect clarity. This visualization must be as though Material when you form it. You also must develop a strong sense of the seven Emotions and learn how to fully become each one. Only when you are able to rapture yourself up within the Emotion will you be able to use your Will at full capacity.

Awareness is developed by watching your thoughts and your environment, and is an in-depth, non-linear understanding of both. You must develop an understanding for what drives you and why it drives you. When you understand why you desire certain things, you will understand why you intend things the way you do, and where your spontaneous images (random thoughts) spring from. You will begin to view the chain within your consciousness that binds you from being aware of your environment, and you will then be able to clearly perceive that as well. To change something in the way you wish it to be, you must first be able to view it as it truly is, rather than in the way you feel about it. This untainted perception is true awareness, and only with its view can Magic be worked.

There are several guidelines for Magic usage that you should ponder. They are:

1. **There is no ultimate evil or good, only better or worse choices for us to make in reference to how we wish things to be.**
2. **Whatever seeds you plant, expect to grow; however, there will always be volunteers living in the garden.**
3. **In regards to any action, always take the course that seems the most simple and feels to be the best.**
4. **If it is, it was meant to be. That which was not meant to be cannot be; this does not mean to not do what you must to change things as you Will.**

5. **The strongest Will is always possessed by the one most passionate on the matter.**
6. **The Shroud dictates the reality and nature of the Material Plane, but we dictate the nature and reality of the Shroud.**
7. **Life is about taking courses in understanding that we have pre-planned for ourselves. Look for the hidden and obvious lessons before attempting to change the way things are.**

When you use these guidelines, you will find your magic possesses a much higher level of potency than you would have thought possible.

Categories of Magic

There are seven different categories of Magic to develop skills in. These are divided by both the ways and types of energies used in order to allow for ease of training in the different categories. Everyone may find some degree of success in all seven of the areas, but it is more likely for you to master one or just a few areas than all seven. Each of our paths will lead us in a different direction to find our lessons, so follow the path you have set out for yourself; you will know this path by listening to your "inner voice" and following what "feels right." Always follow this with your choices and you will feel more satisfied, and be able to work more powerful Magic when you need to do so, regardless of which of the seven areas you are "best" at. The seven categories are: **Conjuring**; **Elemental Magic**; **Emotional Empathics**; **Enchantment**; **Life Magic**; **Perceptive Arts**; and **Spiritism**.

Conjuring is the art of forming the Plane of Imagination strongly enough to attract the awareness of those other than the Conjurer to its being. Using this art is like creating mirages, but it is not sleight-of-hand or stage trickery. The practitioner of this art literally draws the attention of those around him or her to the Images formed in order to mask the Material Plane. Obfuscation, Conjuration of non-Material Manifestations, Lycanthropes and Spectres all fall into the category of this art.

Elemental Magic is the art of directing energy to shape Elemental Manifestations of the Material Plane. This is perhaps the most difficult category of Magic to perform, as the practitioner must be able to either change the Will of the Shroud itself or tear a hole through it. Changing the Shroud or tearing it requires a vast amount of energy and experience, so only the most potent of Shamans will be able to grasp even moderate success in this category. Levitation, True Invisibility, Summoning Energy, State-Changing of Manifestations, and Time Distortion are all included in **Elemental Magic.**

Emotional Empathics is the art of sensing and influencing the Emotional States of other individuals. For a Shaman to master this category, she must have a practical understanding of her own Emotions and responses to them, and also be able to experience Emotions in the same way the individual she is working with will. Zombies, Presenting Auras, Wyrms, and Spirit Healing are the main aspects of this category.

Enchantment is the art of storing Emotions within an Elemental Manifestation or a symbol. This is perhaps the easiest of all the categories of which to obtain a fairly good working grasp. Many of the techniques from this category are also used to enhance those of other categories, therefore it is a very beneficial to train well in **Enchantment.** Charms, Runes, and Fetishes are all part of this category.

Life Magic is the art of directing Life Fire(ether) to animate or repair the state of animation of Material Manifestations. Shamans oriented to Martial or Healing arts will find a lifetime of study and training in this category, for it is well suited in covering nearly all the needs of both. Healing, Resurrection, Ghouls, Golems, and Physical Enhancement are all a part of **Life Magic.**

The Perceptive Arts is the practice of viewing the motion of the energy flow that is existence in order to understand past, present, and future events. Mastery of this category requires a great deal of detachment from the finite perspective of the Material Consciousness, and only those Shamans who are able to free themselves from the

Emotional bindings of the Material Manifestation will be able to find any great deal of success in this area. However, marginal success with quite mysterious answers to questions can be found by most any individual who practices the **Perceptive Arts.** Divination, Scrying, Clairaudience, and Clairvoyance are all included in this category.

Spiritism, the last of the seven categories, is the art of communicating with Spirits by direct awareness to awareness. All Shamans will wish to develop a fair degree of skill in this area, for without it, you will be unable to acknowledge other Spirits to show them respect or to garner respect from them. Summoning, Channeling, Mediumship, and Telepathy are all examples of **Spiritism.**

More in depth information on each of these categories and precise instructions for performing the effects listed will be provided in a later section. Magic and miraculous effects are not the main focus of Shamanism; rather, awareness and understanding are. Without awareness and understanding, which the practice of Follow the Breath will bring to you, you will be unable to gather the energy required to perform even the slightest of effects.

Tools of the Shaman

A Shaman's tools are used for both practical purposes, and also to help gather energy for use in Magic. Tools that are only used for Magic and nothing else tend to clutter up the space required for normal living, so all items a Shaman uses in Magic will be used for day to day needs as well. These tools which are used for Magic are called Foci, for they will assist you in focusing your Will.

For an instrument to help you focus, it must fit you properly. For this reason, it is highly important to select only those that "feel right" to you, and have them as simple or as elaborate as you deem necessary. For one person, drab colors and a simple design may assist in invoking tremendous power, but for another it may take bright fluorescents and complicated etchings to work the same benefit. Select what you deem will be the most proper for you and build upon it, or construct your own from raw materials.

The Blade is a tool of cutting. It should be well maintained, oiled to prevent corrosion, and sharpened with dedicated care. It should be small enough to be carried comfortably, but large enough to slice through the largest of obstacles. This can be a small penknife, sword, or even a dagger of flaked flint. Choose whichever feels proper for you.

The Blade is used in everyday life to slice things, and at times to defend life itself. Slicing is an action of the fine parting the coarse. In Magic, your blade will be used for the same thing; you will use it to draw your subtle energies to a fine point, to carve existence as you Will it to be.

Your Blade will be consecrated by the way you care for it. Each time you sharpen, oil, and polish it, you impart your being into it. This allows you to extend your awareness into it, so that it becomes a part of you. Some are even able to coax non-Material bound Spirits to inhabit their Blades by sharing of Life Fire with them. Either way, care for your Blade in the way you would your own hand, it will grow as a tool of power for you.

The Cloak is a tool of covering that offers protection from the environment. It can be composed of most anything, though the skins of animals who have offered themselves are often found to be the best material for this garment. It should be thick enough to protect against snow, ice, and wind, but light enough to be worn drawn back on the warmer days. Most are hooded. The color of your cloak is unimportant, but the feel of it is of the utmost importance. Make certain your body and Soul both find it comforting, for by this comfort and protection will you be able to draw power with it.

The Cloak in everyday life is used to protect against the environment, and even against attacks. In Magic, it too is used as a kind of armor and buffer from which to draw strength of Spirit. It represents the Shroud and the way it shells the Material Plane. For the Shaman, this is one of the utmost important tools to possess, for it is a sign of the Shaman himself, and also a wonderful protection against the environment itself.

The Cloak is consecrated by the way you feel about it when you wear it, and the way you care for it. The more Emotions of pleasure and security it brings you, the more it will enable you to draw the same into your Magic when you need it to. Care for this as you would your own skin, and it will begin to feel as such; this is also a necessary tool for Lycanthropy.

The Cup is a tool of sustenance. Splendor is not necessary for this item; a simple gourd will suffice. However, this tool, as all others, can be as elaborate as you wish it to be. The shape is inconsequential, as long as it can hold liquids for a long period of time.

This tool is used to provide nourishment for yourself, and to bring together groups of compatriots. By sharing in the Cup, a group can link their Spirits together and weave powerful Magic with one another. This tool is also used to offer gifts to the Unseen Ones and the Spirits; without it, these gifts would simply rest within the soil.

Consecration of the Cup is performed by filling it with Emotions designed to bring togetherness and strength to all who touch it. Drinking the contents will bring the same to the flesh, but merely touching it will bring it to the Soul when you keep the Cup full of this energy. Share it with others frequently, making it known to them that it is designated to bring strength and companionship, and it will grow in power for all who partake of it.

The Pipe is a tool of transformation. This tool can be made from nearly any material; stone, glass, clay, metal and wood pipes are readily available if you do not wish to construct your own. Along with the Pipe is usually carried a Wand, for cleaning the chamber and tamping down the materials which you smoke from it.

This tool is used to transform Sacred Plants by fire into a form absorbable by the body. By inhaling the smoke of the Sacred Plants through the Pipe, you invite their Spirits into yourself as a Deity of Wisdom to empower you and help you gain understanding. This tool is also used to draw together bands of individuals to form one Collective Spirit in which to simply commune, or to work Magic. This tool is also used in ceremony to mark the transition of one Emotion into that of another; an example of this would be partaking in a Pipe with a former enemy to mark the transition into peace.

The Pipe is consecrated, as with the other tools, by the way you care for it. When you construct your own Pipe, more of your Emotions will sink into it. When you share it with others consistently for the same reason, it will begin to take on a deeply residual Emotional vibration, and it will constitute that Emotion into others who partake of the Pipe even when they are not aware of its empowerment. Share this tool with others frequently with an open understanding of what its purpose is, and it will grow in power.

The Pot or **Cauldron** is an iron vessel, in which to brew elixirs, potions, and the Sacred Plants. This tool is also used to prepare food as well, when required. The Pot must be made of iron, for it is durable, easily cleaned, does not typically hold residues or react chemically with any potions or elixirs you may be brewing. Glass is the only other acceptable material from which this can be made, but it is not recommended due to its fragility.

This tool is consecrated with each use, each consecration dependent upon what the specific use is at the time. It should be thoroughly cleansed after each use, to both remove unwanted residues from what was prepared in it, and also to remove the energies placed into whatever was being prepared. It is not unheard of for a Shaman to have several of these dedicated to specific uses; however, a traveling Shaman would not wish to weigh himself down with several of these.

The Pouch and Satchel are container tools used to store and package goods for mobility and organization. Pouches can be used to hold enchanted stones or selections of herbs for various reasons, as well as to carry your Magic Sand in. The Satchel is more of a back-pack, used to carry Pouches and other goods. These items can be used as Foci, but they are more likely to be carrying a Focus Item than to be used as one.

The Staff is the walking stick of the Shaman, and one of the most important Focus Items you will carry. It can be composed of nearly any material, but wood is typically found to be the best material for this item. Chopping down a living tree is not required to obtain your staff; if you walk the forest, you will more likely than not find one lying there as if it were meant for you. These Staffs are the ones possessed of the greatest power, for they are left there by the Unseen Ones and can only be found by a competent Shaman.

In daily living, the Staff is used to brush aside obstacles and assist in areas of poor footing. It is also used for defense against bodily harm, and can be combined with the Blade to create a very effective hunting tool. Your personal staff should be light enough for you to carry with ease and twirl, but heavy enough to hold twice your weight should the need arise.

Many Shamans create rituals designed to empower their Staff with specific attributes. This is not necessary, but it can help in the warding away of malevolent energies directed at you. The Staff is used to help focus the Will of the Shaman in order to summon up a vast quantity of energy for use in Magic; this quantity of Emotion can be so great at times that its sheer bulk is enough to consume energies directed at the Shaman. For this reason, the Staff is one of the Shaman's most powerful tools, as it aids in empowerment and dissolves malicious intents visited upon him.

Music is the most Magical of all the Shaman's tools. Its purpose is to draw together groups of people and inspire them to pour forth certain Emotional Energies, while inhibiting others. With Music, creative expression is encouraged by dance and spontaneous song; this in turn frees the group from stresses and empowers them to work Magic. Music can be generated by many different forms; however, the drum, flute, and voice are the most commonly used by the Shaman.

These are not the only tools used by Shamans for Mundane or Magic purposes; a Shaman should also have a source of fire, mortar and pestle, and other things that are not always completely necessary but extremely helpful. In the working of Magic, use whatever tools help you the most and feel comfortable to you. For the Mundane, do the same. Always use the right tool for the right job no matter what it is, and you will find a much greater ease and success with the work.

The Magic Circle

The Magic Circle is an energetic boundary forming a sphere that is used to enclose an area of the Material Plane in order to separate it distinctively from the rest of that Plane. The Circle itself is the equator of the sphere, and is the focal point when drawing it. This boundary protects both those inside the Circle from the energies without, and those without the Circle from the energies within. Creating the Magic Circle allows you to step slightly away from the Will of the Shroud, thus enabling you to work more powerful Magic.

There are many different techniques prescribed for forming the Magic Circle, and many different incantations and evocations along with those different techniques. Most of these are irrelevant to the actual formation of the Circle itself, and are only incorporated because they allow the Practitioner a greater sense of focus and power when forming their Circle. The only two important things to mind when forming a circle is always move in the Greater Spiral of your hemisphere, and make certain you can feel the energy, if not see its lightning-blue glow as you form the perimeter.

(Whenever a Spiral is observed, there is always a counter-spiral. On the Northern Hemisphere, the Greater Spiral is always clockwise, even in the way the Sun moves through the sky. On the Southern Hemisphere, the Greater Spiral is anti-clockwise. Follow this direction, for the heavier energies will settle in that way, and the lighter will rise upwards in the opposite direction. This is true with all things.)

When you form a Magic Circle in an area, it's generally recommended to begin by facing True North, and starting the Circle in the East, moving in the way which is proper for your hemisphere. However, starting by facing North is not proper for all areas. The sense of ascetics must be correct when you begin drawing a Circle, or you will not be able to "rope off" your area as strongly from the rest of the Material Plane. Also keep in mind that a Magic Circle will remain where you draw it for long after your physical death, and subsequent Circles drawn upon it will thread together as one. When you form a Circle in the same place repeatedly, keep it as close to the way you formed the last one as feels comfortable. This will allow for a more seamless overlap of energies from one Circle to the next.

As you turn, lay down a thick cord of energy until you once again face the direction you began in, and the Circle is closed. At the point the Circle closes, it will become a sphere, taking on the same qualities as the Aura of Spirit, with a bright ball of Ether within the middle, and spiraling vortexes at the northern and southern poles of the sphere. At this point, the Circle is formed and will continue without your Will being applied, as it is a self-sustaining field.

For a more advanced practitioner, it is possible to form a Magic Circle spontaneously by applying pressure where the center of the field will be. This causes a depression in the Earth Aura of the area, rebounding into a spiral and sphere, if you Will it to do so. This approach should only be taken if you are highly experienced in drawing Circles, or if you have a bit of Magic Sand with you.

Magic Sand

Magic Sand is formed by firing sand in your iron vessel until all that can be burned off is gone. Before preparing your fire and vessel, first draw a Magic Circle, and have your sand ready. Sand can be scooped up off the ground for use, or purchased from a garden store. Form your Circle, then light your fire and began to heat the sand, mixing it around in the vessel as it is heated. As smoke pours from the sand, breathe your personal essence into it. From deep within your center, feed your energies into the sand until it begins to breathe with you. Continue doing so for a short while after no more smoke issues from the sand, and you feel it has absorbed all of your essence it is capable of holding. Allow the sand to cool, then place it in your Pouch and seal it up tightly.

This Magic Sand you have formed has many applications, one of them being to form an instant Magic Circle. To form a Circle with the Sand, grab a small amount in your palm, and thrust it downwards with the intention of the essence within the grains bursting forth in an explosion of energy and forming the Circle. This is very similar in technique to forming a Circle without drawing it, and should be used as a primer for the technique itself.

Magic Sand can also be used in healing rituals to help rid ill intent from a targeted individual. Dust the afflicted lightly with sand, instructing them all the while to draw the energies stored within into themselves as a soothingly warm, healing glow. Many times, Wyrms caught within a person will be displaced into the sand during such applications, and the sand can be swept or vacuumed up and returned to the Earth for Emotional purification. Transversely, Magic Sand can also be used to help inflict a person with Wyrms, if Emotions are stirred up by that individual that should be returned to him.

A more mundane use for Magic Sand is in self-defense. Flinging it in the face of an attacker can deter it, be it animal or man, by stinging the eyes. Or more simply, it can be used as part of a "feint of cursing" to allow a would-be attacker to second guess themselves by fear of the unknown. It also makes a great cleaner for your Pot after cooking a meal or preparing a brew. All in all, there are many possible and positive uses for your Magic Sand; be creative in its application, and pour your power into it with its formation.

The Aura

The Aura is a composite field formed of several layers of energy, some static and some highly dynamic. There are four layers to the Aura of a human; two are static, and two are dynamic. The layer of the Spirit and the layer of the Emotional Energy Centers cannot be changed and is therefore considered static. However, the Etheric Aura and the Life Aura are in a constant state of flux, changing constantly in reaction to the environment and with accord to the Emotional Temper of the Individual.

Aura of Spirit

The Aura of Spirit is the unique pattern of Vibration that forms the Individual and gives it distinction from all other Spirits. Contained within the three layers of this Aura is a record of all that has, is, and will be from the perspective of that Spirit. This Aura remains as it was and will be, and cannot change without the Spirit becoming a distinctly different individual. This is perhaps the most difficult Aura to view, and it is possible that only those who are One with All may glimpse it.

Emotional Energy Centers

Emotional Energies are bands of energy that travel in wave-like patterns, formed of a combination of the Three Vibrations. The Emotional Energy Centers are points that resonate with the seven Emotional Energies. Though these Centers never change their frequency, the bands stretching between them, which govern Emotional Temper, do change. There are seven Emotional Energy Centers, and from these Emotions are manifest.

The Crown Point Center vibrates with the frequency of **Compassion.** Its appearance is of **Silver** or simple brilliance. This Center is said to be the seat of **Enlightenment**, and is the key to the First Plane. Its dominant day is **Saturday.**

The Third Eye Center vibrates with the frequency of **Elation.** It appears as **Purple** or one of its shades. This Center is the seat of **Clairvoyance,** and is the key to the Second Plane. **Sunday** is its dominant day.

The Throat Center vibrates with the frequency of **Fear.** It appears as **Blue**, and is the seat of **Telepathy.** This Center is the key to the Third Plane, and **Monday** is its dominant day.

The Heart Center is home of the **Love/Hate Fixation.** It appears as **Green.** This Center is the seat of **Projection.** It is the key to the Fourth Plane. **Tuesday** is its dominant day.

The Center of the Solar Plexus vibrates with the frequency of **Courage.** It appears as **Yellow** or gold. This is the seat of **Telekinesis.** It is the key to the Fifth Plane, and is dominant upon **Wednesday.**

The Abdominal Center vibrates with the frequency of **Anxiety,** and appears as **Orange.** This is the seat of **Alchemy**, and the key to the Sixth Plane. **Thursday** is its dominant day.

The Root Center vibrates with the frequency of **Malice**, and appears **Red** in color. It is the seat of **Pyrogenesis**. It is the key to the Seventh Plane, and is dominant upon **Friday.**

Corresponding with each of these Emotional Energy Centers is also a musical chord, consisting of the same note from seven septaves. The sound of the first is A, the second B, et cetera. It should also be noted that the exact tone of both sound and color is not precisely identical to its Material Plane representation, as these qualities are not Material.

Etheric Aura

The Etheric Aura is a field composed of energies pulled to, held in check by, and pushed away from a person's center by that individual's Emotional Temper. It cycles through phases of waxing and waning, varying with situations each individual encounters on multiple planes. The base form of Ether, also known as Quintessence or the Fifth Element, is that of a lukewarm, watery gelatin with a faint electric-blue color. However, when influenced by Emotional Energies and circulating as an individual's aura, it can take on an almost innumerable quantity of qualities which differ from its typical state.

The Etheric Aura begins at the center in a highly dense point. At times this point expands or contracts, dependent upon both the Emotional State of the individual and the quantity of Ether they are able to attract versus expend. At its most minute, the center point will appear as a dim seed, and at its grandest it will appear as a watery ball which glows from within. This center is a stationary point in the Etheric Aura in comparison with the rest; however, it is not static and the Ether is constantly refreshed.

Moving to the North and the South of the center point, vortex funnels which serve three purposes can be found. These vortexes are formed by the constant inhale and exhale of Ether at the center point, and not only do they both move energies in a dual manner to and away from the center, but their gyrations turn the currents of the field itself, achieving a balance of Emotionally-charged Ether. Energies inhaled at the Northern vortex spiral downwards clockwise, and at the Southern the inhaled spiral upwards anti-clockwise. Expelled energies from both of these vortexes travel out in the opposite spiral from each respectively, and tend to continue on in a stream for a short distance before dissipating.

As the Northern vortex drives its hemisphere clockwise, the Southern vortex drives its in opposition. This causes the Ether to roll against itself at the equator of the Etheric Aura, but it does not bulge the field as one might suppose. Rather, a belt of Ether is formed just above the main bulk of the field which spirals in a double-helix shape which encirculates the rest of the Aura. In other places around the Aura, (which may change shape and position,) spherical swirls of Ether also formed by opposing currents which are similar to the Auric Belt may be found.

The outlying edge of the Etheric Aura can appear in three ways: fading away, ending abruptly, and ending with a very dense "skin." Each of these three ways is associated with a specific state of Emotional dominance, which regulates how much

Ether is held and in what way it is held. The most desirable condition for the edge of your field is the "thick skin," for it helps to contain a greater amount of Ether, which then fuels your Life Fire and your Magic abilities. This skin is also more repulsive to invasions by Wyrms and Auric Tendrils, which are caught up and absorbed into the thick check point rather than able to penetrate the Aura to change it or rob it of Ether.

The density and quality of the Etheric Aura is directly related to the Emotional State of the individual. Emotional State refers to Tempering, or the way a person resonates in response to both other Emotions and environment encounters. There are natural responses in order to both achieve balance and to secure one's life. When you experience someone in distress, for instance, the natural reaction is to calm their distress, for to do otherwise would allow their distress to resonate through you and increase this feeling in both of you. This is because their distress disperses their energies, and it will take yours along with it if you resonate this Emotion. However, when you encounter a merry person you will also be inclined to feel merry because this draws energies in to yourself. In regards to the merry individual, some will at times resonate with him, and others at times will resonate against him. This occurs both because of balance and because of unresolved Emotionally generative issues. It is important to the practice of Magic and as a Shaman that you understand why you react to any Emotion in the way you do, and precisely what Emotion you are responding with. The Emotion a person resonates is typically seen not for the Emotion itself, but for the results of the Emotion. For instance, Emotions closer to the Heart Center tend to hold Ether and other Emotions in check, resulting in a more static Aura that does not flow easily away or attract more Ether to itself; whereas Emotions nearer to the Root Center tend to cause an Aura and other energies in general to leap outwards and dissipate quickly. There are also body changes in response to the way your Etheric Aura moves about that can be used to determine which Emotion is being experienced. The most sure way to gain a firm understanding of your Emotional Temper and of the way to balance it is by following your breath daily.

Life Fire Aura

As Ether is pulled into the body, it transforms into a "flame" which binds the awareness of the Spirit to the flesh. This flame is called Life Fire, and it is this which animates the Material Manifestation of Spirits. This flame encapsulates the body and flows through it by means of a complex system of channels, reservoirs, and portals.

By perceiving this Aura and adjusting its circulation, a Shaman can keep himself and others free from illness, and help to recuperate from injuries much more swiftly. This is the basis for such health practices as Acupuncture and Qigong, and only by working directly with this Aura can the body be healed holistically. Illness begins with an irregularity in the flow of Life Fire through the body, so detecting it and correcting it before it becomes an injury can save much pain and recovery time. It is also possible to achieve such a mastery over this system that the body can be sustained without nourishment such as air, food, and water for extended periods of time or endure extremes of cold and heat.

There are two sources of Life Fire within the human energy system. One is the original vitality received at conception, and the other is by the assimilation of nutrients gained from the consumption of other living entities. Assimilating nutrients is a chemically complex process which requires air, minerals, and water and increasing Life Fire by this source tends to lead the body on a slow decay process known as aging, which ultimately ends at death when the original vitality is completely used up. Increasing the original vitality is a completely different process of cultivating Life Fire than assimilating nutrients; it requires a strict regulation of energy expenditures by thought and intake of supplemental nutrients as well as the daily performance of yogic internal alchemy processes. The overall ease of simply consuming to live, even though the span of life will be drastically shortened, is a temptation many are all too willing to indulge in rather than strike out on the life-long quest of vital cultivation. For this reason, much of the knowledge on how to perform internal alchemy has been forgotten, lost, or scoffed into hiding over the ages. It is important that you should know the difference between the two methods, so that you will have the option to choose which way you wish to survive.

Despite which method of Life Fire cultivation you practice, Ether is constantly inhaled into the body to be transmuted to this spiritually-binding substance. This Ether enters into the body most strongly through certain areas such as the sacrum, crown point of the head, third eye region of the brow, palms of the hands and soles of the feet. It is also through these points that Ether, and at times even Life Fire, exits the body with great flow. The conscious direction of the inhaling aspect of absorbing Ether is practiced traditionally by Eastern Shamans through an exercise called "Five Gates Breath."

Five Gates Breath Exercise

The practice of Five Gates Breath optimally should become a non-stop effort. When first practicing, begin in the early part of your day when you feel well rested and you have already limbered out and eaten. It is also not wise to begin practicing this exercise while communing with the Sacred Plants or under the influence of alcohol. To practice Five Gates Breath:

1. Stand with your feet shoulder width apart, with your body relaxed and your arms at your side.

2. Settle your breath deep into your abdomen, taking care not to inhale to complete lung capacity as this induces tension in the ribcage. Also do not attempt to control your breathing; after deepening it to your abdomen, allow the pace of your breath to set itself. Always inhale through the nose, and exhale through the mouth.

3. Expand your awareness to your immediate environment and self. Settle your thoughts as you do when you Follow the Breath.

4. Shift your awareness to your forehead, palms, and the soles of your feet. As you inhale, feel in each of these five areas for the draft of Ether. This feels almost as though you were inhaling air through these areas. If you have difficulty with sensing the influx of energy, begin practicing solely with your dominant hand until it becomes sensitive, and then expand the practice to the other five areas. It is acceptable and encouraged to practice with each one

individually if you feel you need to do so, and especially when you are having difficulty with any one area.

5. Continue practicing this at the very least daily for one half hour. As stated previously, you will wish to build up this practice until it is constant. Seven days before your natural death, you will not inhale through these gates without conscious effort; therefore, it is wise for anyone who wishes to pursue a long life to practice this exercise consistently and constantly. Applying so much effort in this exercise will also enable you access to a vast store of energy that those who neglect this exercise will not be privy to, in both physical and Magical fields.

The Life Fire Aura tends to extend outwards from the body, tracing its contour as it radiates from the skin. This aura generally appears to be a pale green color, though it can be so transparent at times to appear completely clear. It is through the perception and adjustment of this field that Shamans are able to assist others with healing their body and diagnosing maladies. Whenever a person is affected by an illness or injury, it is shown here by the way the field gravitates towards the injured area. Life Fire will always flow towards damaged areas of the body in order to replace the diminished energy in the area. By manipulating the quantity and quality of Life Fire in these damaged areas, instantaneous or rapid repair can be produced.

Auric Tendrils

Auric Tendrils are extensions of the Etheric Aura, wisped about by the Will. These can have many functions, from simply feeling out another person to exchanging energies with them. These Tendrils are mainly extended without a person's awareness when conversing with or thinking about another person. However, there are other individuals who have developed a grand degree of control over these in order to effect changes in the Etheric and Life Fire Auras of others.

Psychic Vampires are masters of draining the Auric fields of others. Their tactic is simple: Will the energy of another into their own field to sustain it. A few Vampires do consciously form tendrils in order to drain their victims, but most are not Spiritually developed enough to understand that is the mode of transfer. The tendrils they unleash have sharp points which strike about half way into their victim's Aura, and then curl around into a hook or a barb to hold in. These tendrils then work like tubes, guiding the Ether and Life Fire from the victim into the Vampire.

Often, the Vampire's grasp is forcibly retracted by fleeting attention which rips the tied-down tendrils apart, stuck in the victim's Aura. This results in gashes in the Aura of the victim, especially if the victim doesn't practice with his or her energy system. In time, depending on the Etheric replenishment methods of the victim, the gashes will close up and disappear. However, if the victim has poor replenishment methods, the broken off tendrils will reach out from his Aura and attach themselves to others, changing the victim into a Vampire.

The Shaman uses Auric Tendrils in the reverse method of the Vampire. Instead of leeching and leaving, the Shaman will manipulate sections of Ether which are impregnated with "harmful" Emotions and transmute them into "clean" energies, sometimes first pulling them within his own body. Or in the case of a physical wound, the Shaman will direct his own Life Fire along with that of the injured party's into the damaged area in order to effect a more rapid recovery.

Whenever dealing with an injured party, do not begin by trying to suck away the stagnation. Instead, you should begin by fueling their system with Ether. This is performed by imaging a lightning bolt of Ether flow from one of your Five Gates into the injured person's Aura. You will know naturally where it needs to be applied as you perform this. As you continue pouring energy into them, the energies that need to be transmuted will flow into you. Depending upon the nature of the disorder, these will appear as a brilliant or deep-hued red color, but this is not always the case. After all the "bad stuff" has flowed into your energy system, you must now transmute it into an inert form. Many Shamans do this by placing it in mucous or into the digesting contents of the stomach, then vomit it out to allow the energy a chance to break down and rejoin the environment. For some, this method is reflexive, and if so it should be the one followed. For the others, you must take the harmful energies now in your system and directly change them into either a sheer brilliant clarity, or a deep electric-blue color. This method takes out the scattering Emotional charge, and returns it to either gathering Emotions, or simply reverts it back to uncharged Ether. Whether you vomit it out for energetic compost or Will it to an inert form, the energies must not be allowed to stay in your system as they are when they entered it.

Treating a Vampire is a bit more different than treating his victim. A Vampire must be first instructed on how to reap Ether from the Earth and the Cosmos, or a heal cannot be effected. Once the Vampire has shown proficiency in the technique of gathering energy from the Earth, you may begin to influence their energy system and close the rifts within it.

The rifts in the energy system are created by Light Emotions (which push away.) These Emotions were necessary to move the Ether from one energy system into another; however, they will continue to dispel spots of an Aura if the system is not regularly balanced. The Ether you will fill these spots with should feel "sticky" to you; this is charged with Sound Emotion and it will hold itself in place. When working with rifts in the Aura of any individual, use many small "sparks" of Ether flowing from your offhand palm, and with your primary palm pull up a solid stream of Ether from the ground. The Ether you are utilizing to repair their Aura should not come directly from your system, but should be channeled from the ground into them. The Earth's Aura is properly tuned at the perfect frequency our own Auras should be operating at, and drawing up it's Ether will balance out their entire system.

Earth and Cosmic Auras

Every Celestial Body has an Etheric Aura of its own. Each of these Auras is perfectly tuned for itself and constantly balancing out to where it need be. These Celestial Auras also sends out tapers, or streams, of energy into Deep Space which shower down upon other Celestial Bodies and become transmuted into a part of that

Body's Aura, and sent out again to rain down upon another Star or Planet. This is the basic principle behind the practice of Astrology, and the reason for its effectiveness at predicting human Emotional States during different alignments, as the process of transmuting differently-tinged energies off-balances the human system.

The Etheric Aura of the Earth is almost precisely identical to the same system within a human, except on a much-more massive scale. Like the small currents of Ether which balance in the human system, the Earth's Aura has Ley Lines, which are huge currents of force. There are also spots in the Earth's Aura which are either "dead zones"- areas where the Ether has been stagnant for quite a while or is inhaled into the earth in massive quantities, or vortexes which pour energy into the cosmos in great abundance. Many religious sites were built on these vortexes in order to take advantage of the "fresh" Ether flowing into the Cosmos there. Upon these vortexes, the Emotional charge of the Ether cannot be easily changed and its quantity depleted. Unfortunately, we cannot all have a vortex on which to meditate without first forming it.

Forming a vortex involves first of all the ability to view Ether without difficulty. You must be able to see and feel the way it flows from the Earth in the vicinity, so that you are able to tell if you will be disturbing a natural process by forming this vortex. It is unwise to form a grand vortex in a dead zone. This tends to make the energy state of the area change very dramatically very swiftly, and can upset the balance of your Etheric Aura enough to knock you physically unconscious. Forming a vortex directly upon a Ley Line is also unwise and unneeded. The area of a Ley Line is constantly replenished with energy, and forming a vortex directly upon the line will channel its Ether into the cosmos and create a new dead zone where the Ether should have been flowing to. Drastically upsetting the Earth's Aura is unnecessary and it will cause a backlash of balance in time.

When you form a vortex, it both inhales energy from the Cosmos and releases the Earth Ether into the cosmos at once. These small vortexes, when placed with caution and precision, actually help balance out the Earth's Aura by shifting a bit of flow away from the more massive vortexes like the Bermuda Triangle in the Caribbean, the Devil's Triangle in the Pacific, and several other land-bound vortexes spanning the globe. Begin to form your vortex by pulling down Ether from the Cosmos, and pulling up Ether from the Earth. These two should intertwine, forming a double-spiral or helix no larger than the size of your thigh. As these two energies mate with one another, an indention will impress itself upon the Earth Aura and bowl upwards to accept the Cosmic Ether. Cosmic Ether will fill this bowl and turn deosil (sun-wise; clockwise, for the Northern Hemisphere and anti-clockwise for the Southern Hemisphere) while the Earth Ether which forms the bowl turns the opposite direction. Once the bowl is formed, you have shaped a vortex.

A Shaman-formed vortex requires maintenance as dictated by the flow of energies in the area. Some areas will support a vortex indefinitely, while others will only sustain them for a few moments. Regardless of this, the longer a vortex is held in place, the more likely it is that the Etheric flow of the area will adapt itself to sustain the vortex. When you form a vortex, continue moderating it over the next few years and it will become semi-permanent and remain for generations without maintenance.

Vortexes are known to attract Unseen Ones and Spirits who come to bathe in the energies. They are also considered to be highly regarded gifts to the same, and a most beneficial addition to any Sacred Space you form to work magic in. When seeking to attract Spirits, doing so at a vortex will most often give you better results. If you meditate or work at a vortex which is known for its Spirits, make certain to leave gifts for them out of respect. In the Spirit world, respect given is respect returned.

Circulating the Etheric Aura

Developing sensitivity to the feel, sight, and sound of the Etheric Aura can be difficult for many for they attempt to see what they imagine an Aura should look like instead of simply perceiving what is there. A simple exercise to increase your perception of Ether and your own Aura is to consciously circulate your Etheric Aura. Sensations of this always begin with the feel of it, then sight follows, and once you become adept you will even gain enough sensitivity to hear it. This exercise also increase the amount and vigor of Ether within your Aura and should be practiced daily if only for a few moments by any Shaman who wishes a great degree of stamina in Magic practices.

1. Begin this exercise by sitting comfortably with legs crossed. No advanced seating positions are necessary for this exercise to be successful. In this exercise, state of mind and Will is much more important than state of body or body position.

2. Relax yourself and breath deep into your abdomen. Allow your breath to settle itself and do not attempt to control its pattern once it has deepened. Relaxation of body and breath is important, for each exhale will help you drive your Aura with more impetus.

3. Turn the perception of your Third Eye inwards to find the center of your Etheric Aura. This center is found in the Solar Plexus region of the body. It may be easier for some to look for the effects of the center, which feels like a dense ball of gel, rather than for the center itself. The current of force which flows directly around the center turns very slowly and feels heavy. Seek out this sensation, then follow it outwards.

4. Once you have found your center, follow the currents to the edge of your field. You will find that with dedicated practice, you will be able to perceive the currents completely around you at once, rather than viewing it in pieces as you would with normal vision. Establish for yourself a feel for the pace of the currents and the distance from the center to the edge of the field. If you can see it, examine it to gain an understanding of how it flows normally. Without this understanding, increasing it will be very difficult.

5. After gaining a full view of your Etheric Aura, push its currents from the center. If you are in the Northern Hemisphere, to clockwise put the effort, and if in the Southern, the opposite holds. Keep in mind that the entire Aura will turn both directions simultaneously, but it is easier to follow the gathering spin of your hemisphere. With each exhale, push your Aura. With each inhale, relax. Do not attempt to force it; always be gentle when working with the Ether. If you do not have enough sensitivity to push it easily, you will not push it anymore if you try to force it. Forcing it also consumes a vast amount of the Ether you have stored in your body for conversion to Life Fire, and even Life Fire itself.

6. When you gain the ability to see the Etheric Aura with little difficulty, you will notice it brightens significantly when you turn it. This is because the energy is compacting itself, and you are gathering more within your field. Once you are able to hear it, you will notice it moves with a "whoosh" sound that also increases and decreases. Extremely adept individuals will notice that along with the "whoosh" is a sound reminiscent of an almost infinite number of small bells tinkling, similar to wind chimes. The sound of song within the Aura is a sign of Etheric Mastery.

7. Finish this exercise when you feel satisfied that you have practiced satisfactorily for the time being, and then gently stretch out your body. This helps to ground the energies you have gathered and works well to prevent stiff joints during future sittings. Practice this exercise whenever you feel the need, but do not force yourself if you do not feel as though you should.

Personal Vortex

A variation on the Auric Circulation exercise is known as the Personal Vortex. This technique allows you to convert Cosmic Ether into Earth Ether through your own Auric Field. It also constructs a nearly-impenetrable shield against unwanted Emotions and Tendrils, but not by repulsion of these energies. Rather, this technique shields by way of transmutation, the Alchemy of Spirit.

1. Begin this exercise by performing Auric Circulation. However, in this practice you will not simply circulation your Aura, but you will also begin to

pull Ether into it consciously through the Northern and Southern Vortexes. The Northern Vortex will inhale Cosmic Ether, and the Southern will inhale Earth Ether. Begin by coinciding your pulls with your breathing, but increase the draw until you inhale through both constantly.

2. Expand your Auric Center as you inhale, drawing the two energies through it. Cosmic Ether must become Earth Ether as it passes through the center, and Earth Ether must become Cosmic Ether.

3. As you expand your center, draw the quantity of Cosmic and Earth Ethers towards each other, until the grind forcefully against one another. Continue pulling the one to the other until the Earth Ether reaches your Northern Vortex, and the Cosmic Ether reaches your Southern Vortex, thus encapsulating your Aura.

4. At the moment of encapsulation, expand your center to the far reaches of your field to cover the Cosmic and Earth Ethers, thus catching them. Continue rotating your Aura throughout this whole exercise.

5. Once you have grasped the two Ethers with your Center, grab your entire Aura and crush it back downwards into its center. All of the Cosmic, Earth, and your own Ether must be drawn inwards. Compress these energies until they seem to disappear, at which point they will combust and explode back outwards.

6. Your Aura will be thin for the next few days. Practice Five Gates Breath and Auric Circulation as much as possible until it is replenished. This exercise need only to be performed once when done properly, but it may take several

attempts to find success. End this exercise as you would Auric Circulation, by stretching out and taking a short walk.

Differing Magic Spells from Magic Ritual

Spells and Rituals are two different approaches to manipulating energies to perform Magic. Spells are typically associated with Witches, while Rituals are typically associated with Wizards. The reason for this association stems from the traditional ways in which both of these Path distinctions are taught to manipulate currents of force by focus items. However, this association is not a necessarily correct or advantageous view for one who wishes to be able to utilize both of these powerful techniques in their own workings. To use Spells and Rituals to their fullest extent, you must grasp an understanding of what gives the one distinctiveness from the other and where their advantages and weaknesses lie.

The Magic Spell

The Magic Spell is a quick and often spontaneous motivation of energies in order to perform an effect. The focus when performing a Spell is to allow the energies that perform the transformation you call for to completely consume your being (or your Awareness/Consciousness.) "Firing off" a Spell requires a high degree of Emotion; this is an advantage and a weakness at the same time. You must be deeply, deeply involved with the ends of the effect to the point that it is as though your very existence depends upon what you are performing. There also must be no resistance on your part of anything that feels natural for you to do as part of the Spell. If you feel like screaming or crying, stripping down naked or rolling around on the ground, those things must be done to fully empower the Spell. A Spell is completed when all the motivating energies have been drained from you, and its memory should fade for a time after you perform it, but only if you resist no part of it.

A Spell cannot be planned out beforehand. It is highly potent Magic that seems to tear from the Shaman, directing the Shaman to perform it as it performs itself. Though this type of Magic cannot be scheduled, there are practitioners who are capable of unleashing this intensity at Will through much determined training aimed at allowing the Shaman to understand himself and gather Ether. This training cannot be taught from one to another, just as the specifics of working a Spell cannot be instructed to another; it is developed by the process of unraveling the knots of the internal/external world view.

When you feel the urge to direct currents come upon you, no matter what it may seem to be, follow it. Put up no resistance to motions or vocalizations so long as they injure no one including yourself. (Injurious urges towards self or others are NOT a part of the normal Spell spontaneity, and if felt, the Spell should be halted immediately.) Once the "Spirit" has left you, eat a bit and rest, do not speak of the matter for at least three days, and do not inquire of it with thoughts or actions.

The Magic Ritual

The Magic Ritual is all about the process. It must be precisely planned and perfectly orchestrated. In a Ritual, every component up to the steps you take will have meaning in order to draw in energy. The Emotions for the Will in a Ritual are drawn from components. A little is taken from the Circle cast, and from the cloaking of the practitioner; a little from the scent of the burning incense and from the dancing light of the fire. Rituals are delicate weavings of energy requiring intricacy and skill.

Powerful Rituals are highly Ceremonial, often practiced many times before the occasion, and timed out precisely to the most beneficial astronomical positions possible. Rituals are often called upon when little Emotion towards the effect intended are present, as the energies can be stirred very powerfully by a combination of focus items and techniques such as chanting and gesturing. Strong Emotions towards an effect can also be woven very successfully into a Ritual, which will enhance the direction of the energies motivated towards the goal. A wise Shaman will practice with tools and techniques so that he develops an understanding of what works best for him within a Ritual working.

Rituals are also used for group healing sessions. A Shaman may use a Spell to work with a person one-on-one, but it does not allow the one being healed to interact very much with the Shaman in the process of healing and tends to leave a feeling of dependency upon the Shaman for health with the injured party. However, when in a Ritual setting, the Shaman helps the person to be healed to understand that ultimately, it is their responsibility to heal themselves and only they have the true power to do so. In this way, healing in Rituals is a much more beneficial process.

When performing a Ritual, plan well ahead. Research astronomical charts and positions and see which Celestial Bodies will best benefit your work. Work when these Celestial Bodies shine upon you, so that you can use their energies directly. If you will use poetry or prose, have these scripted prior to and practiced until you can flawlessly speak them. Know what tools you will use and have them prepared for days ahead of time, along with your space and altar, as much as you possibly can. Make certain that all of your close compatriots know not to disturb you at this time, but do not tell them specifics on what you are doing. If you choose to disclose information to anyone not participating in the Ritual with you, wait at least a few days after the Ritual to do so.

Keep Your Own Counsel

Whether working a Spell or a Ritual, keep your own counsel on your idea of degree of success and what you had in mind to begin with. Sharing with others simply to promote the idea that you work Magic can instill non-beneficial Emotions in them in reference to you that will at best hinder your Magic and at worst end your life. Conversing with another practitioner in order to share ideas and gain understanding is helpful, but simply speaking to gratify your sense of ego will cause problems for you.

Transcendence From Material Consciousness

The physical form and its three needs of comfort, nourishment, and sex bind the Consciousness to the Seventh Plane of Existence. Spirituality and Shamanism begin by first understanding the nature of these chains, and then continue through the process of freeing the Consciousness from them. This process of unbinding produces what are typically referred to as "Altered States of Consciousness," for they move your Awareness from the Material to the Spiritual.

Sanity is the "Normal State of Consciousness," which is only concerned with the three Carnal necessities and modes of acquiring more of them. It is natural to be drawn to this state of mind, for without it we would be unable to maintain a Material existence. However, the Spirit requires that one draw their Consciousness away from the Sane and into the realm of the Insane; any actions taken that do not reward with some form of the three Carnal Needs could most definitely and rightly so be considered Insane. This is why "Altered States" are highly prized by all Paths of the Spirit. For the Shaman, a balance must be struck between the Sane and the Insane or it is not possible to walk with the Spirits.

Delusions and hallucinations are forms of Altered States of Consciousness in which the delusional individual cannot differentiate between the Material Plane and the Plane of Imagination. Many of these individuals do not just see their own formations of the Plane of Imagination; they will also see its formations presented by Spirits and other humans as well as its natural landscape. Hallucinations are seeing bits of Imagination as tangible as Material, whereas delusions are experiencing nearly if not the entire landscape as though it is Material. It is not the goal of the Shaman to hallucinate or become delusion, though Visions are highly sought after and more prized than any of the Carnal Needs themselves. The Shaman must be able to distinguish between the Planes at all times, especially when employing Altered States to free himself from the chains of Materialism.

There are Altered States of Consciousness which bind one to the Carnal. These States are intentionally employed to bind to the Material by presenting a sense of fulfillment of the Carnal Needs. Examples of modes of inducing these Altered States are: entertainment, recreational substance use, and abuse of eating and sex. Compulsive eating, exercise, and sex along with many artistic mediums are the most commonly used modes found today. These same mediums can be turned to free the Consciousness, but it is all reliant upon each person's motivation to approach it in that way to do so. Passivity in Altered States will almost always lead to more binding rather than unchaining.

Meditation is perhaps one of the most-utilized techniques to free the mind from the Carnal, but it is only a beginning. This first step should be used to first understand how you have chained yourself so that you can see where to unlock yourself first. Along with this, regulation of the Carnal Needs should also be employed. Deprivation and denial of the Carnal Needs can be used to achieve Altered States, but this is unhealthy to the Material Manifestation and can lead to death in certain circumstances. For this reason, it is discouraged. After Meditation, the most successful and least dangerous mode of achieving Altered States is by the use of the Sacred Teacher Plants. With these you have the added benefit of guidance of the Plant Spirits when you have shown them the proper quantity of respect required to attract their nurturance. As with other activities and substances, there is abuse potential in the Sacred Teacher Plants, but this same potential is present in any activity you participate in.

The Material Manifestation cannot leave the Material Plane, as the Material Consciousness of the Seventh Plane cannot leave the Material Manifestation. In order to access the other Six Planes of Existence, Awareness must move freely between the state of being, or Consciousness, inherent to each Plane. Before we took this Material form, we freely moved through the Planes. However, upon garbing ourselves in flesh, we lost all memory of this and most of the knowledge of how to do this. The Planes become new to us again, and we can become lost in them and frightened.

The Plant Spirits and other Familiar Spirits are more than happy to assist us in our experiencing of stumbling the Planes anew, when we have shown them respect and gratitude for their willingness to do so. This is why the Plants have offered us keys to reaching Altered States, and medicines with those keys. Exploring the Planes can be done without the guidance of the Spirits, but it can be egotistically treacherous for us to do so, as what we experience (without remembering we have experienced this before) can drastically change our perspectives on ourselves and the world around us. Failing to give the proper respect (for you show respect in all things you do) will tend to incline the Spirits to show the same regard for you.

Holy Days of the Shaman

Holy Days (holidays) of the Shaman are aligned with astronomical events. These events mark processions of change and times when certain energies are more influential than others. There are many astronomical events, some of which occur only such a great passage of time that they may not be observed in your lifetime. Major Holy Days of the Shaman are the Equinoxes, the Solstices, and the Full and New Lunar Phases. All of the Holy Days of the Shaman are celebrated with a Communion by the Sacred Teacher Plants.

Vernal Equinox

The Vernal Equinox, or Spring Equinox, appears in the second third of the month of March. It is hailed as a day of Ceremony to welcome the return of Spirits into Material Manifestations, and as the Shaman's New Year. The Shaman takes this occasion to welcome Spirits who have returned to the 7th Plane, and to share blessings of protection with the young of all Plants and Animals who nurture and provide sustenance for one another in the Cycle. Festivals of the Vernal Equinox involve the sharing of tribal(or local) lore, a feast of the early spring vegetation, and the introduction of others into the powers of Magic. This is a particularly potent time for conversation with the Spirits of Nature.

Summer Solstice

The Summer Solstice is the longest span of daytime during the course of the year, and as such, it is reserved for celebration of the Sun and its intense, life-nurturing energies. This event appears in the second third of the month of June, and is celebrated with a feast of summer vegetations and livestock. The Shaman takes this occasion to absorb as vast a quantity of the Sun's Ether as possible. This occasion is highly potent for treating those with chronic or severe ailments. Shamans often use the Summer Solstice to introduce their apprentices to visionary experiences and the other Planes by way of the Sacred Plants.

Autumnal Equinox

The Autumnal Equinox appears in the second third of the month of September. This event is celebrated to honor the Spirits who have left their Material Manifestations and await a return to the Cycle. Festivals of this Equinox involve costumes, singing and dancing, and a feast consisting of harvest foods and wild game. The Shaman uses this time to help guide Spirits who have left the Cycle through the Planes, and to an understanding of why they must release the Emotions held over from their Material Manifestations. This time is most potent for conversation with the deceased as they were when alive.

Winter Solstice

The Winter Solstice appears in the second third of the month of December. This Solstice is dedicated to the Moon, as it is the longest night of the year. It is celebrated with gift-giving, a feast of grains and wild game, and a candle-light observance of the event. The Shaman prizes this occasion for the absorbance of Lunar Ether. The Winter Solstice is a potent time for divinations and Scrying into the past, present, and future. For the Apprentice Shaman, this is a time of testing, for he must seek a vision into the truth of himself.

Full Moon

The Full Moon is a time of high influence upon Earth by Lunar Ether. The abundance of this energy allows for a more easy application of many types of Magic, and for more clarity in Divinations and Scrying. Observances of this event vary by necessity and the personal tastes of the observers. It occurs approximately every 29 days.

New Moon

The New Moon, or Dark Moon is a phase during which the Ether transmuted by the Moon and directed at the Earth is at its lowest. During this phase of the Lunar Cycle, the Earth Ether and Ether from the other Celestial Bodies is at its most potent. This is a perfect time for aligning yourself with the steady flow of Earth Ether and gathering its most-nurturing-of-all energies into yourself. As with the Full Moon, observances of this event vary by necessities in Magic and by the personal tastes of the observers.

Other Events

There are many other astronomical events which bring changes of energy currents with them. These range from the passage of comets, to meteor showers, to planetary alignments. Only detailed astrological charts(which are planned much farther into the future than astronomical charts,) will be able to show the full array of events and an idea of what type of energies they bring with them. An important event to note will occur on December 21, 2012, during which it is said our Sun will align with the gravitational equator of our Galaxy for the first time in several millennia. This event will be held in special regard the world over; how you choose to observe it is up to you.

Minerals and Magic

Celestial Bodies affect Ether by transmuting it. This transmuted energy then flows out into the Cosmos to rain down upon all other Celestial Bodies and their inhabitants. This is the Magic of the Stars and the Earth, but few realize that crystals, metals, and other minerals work in the same way as the Celestial Bodies which they compose.

There is no more inherent power in one crystal or mineral than there is in any other. The simple difference between them in context of Magic is the way they transmute energies. There are many interpretations to the way minerals react in response to different types of energy. A detailed listing of every mineral and its transmutative abilities could fill several volumes, and so they will not be included here for sake of reference. Rather, you should work with minerals and feel for yourself how they work for you. The abilities of each will respond differently to different individuals. Detailed listings make for interesting reading material, but they cannot provide you with working knowledge on how to use the minerals you have at hand. Experiment with your stones by influencing them with different flavors of energy, and see how they respond to you. In this way, you will gain experience and an understanding of how each stone you possess works for you.

Raising Energy for Effects

All Magic is performed by strong Emotion to push the work; concise Imaging of what you wish to perform; and sufficient Ether to transmute and perform the change. There are as many methods of gathering Ether and Emotion as there are practitioners of Magic. You must find the mode which works the best for you; experimentation with tools and techniques is highly advisable if you wish to develop proficiency in the Arts.

Generally speaking, any technique that allows you to form a clear view of the Ether you are working with and "massage" it into shape will lead to success. Singing, dancing, playing music, and dedicated hand motions are all very simple ways of helping you motivate and view the energy. These techniques should never be used out of tradition only in Magic; only when they are dedicated to the purpose of motivating Ether to the point that you can see, feel, and hear it will they be successful. Chanting "magic words" is ineffective if you are not motivating energy with them. There is no Magic or power in words except what you place into them. Always remember that ultimately, no technique will bring you power; it is you who must bring power to the technique.

For success in the following instructions in Magic, practice. Be inventive and do not be afraid to experiment. Follow what you feel to be the proper course of action, and do not regret. If you come to a point where you are unsure as to which action you should take, take the action that you feel most strongly compelled towards, despite any worries to the contrary.

Though a thousand lives you may live, you live each one only once. Keep your Magic alive!

Section 3:

The Sacred Teacher Plants

All Things Being Sacred

Certain plants and mushrooms are referred to as being sacred, but it should be noted that these are in truth no more sacred than any other part of existence. All things are One, joined together through all the Seven Planes of Existence. Because of this unity of existence, for one bit to be sacred means that the entire lot is sacred. Despite this, certain plants and fungi are termed sacred beyond the others due to their ability to liberate us from the bonds we have imposed upon ourselves through perception, and to help free us to roam the Planes where Material cannot be found.

To maintain our Material Manifestations, there must be a transfer of material from one form to the next. This transfer in and of itself is also considered sacred; when a plant pulls up minerals from the earth and light from the sun, the essence of their spirits becomes one with the essence of the Plant Spirit. When an animal passes and consumes part of the plant, the fused essences within the plant likewise further mix into the Animal Spirit that consumed it. Then, we humans devour the animal, and our Spirit is forged together with the essences that made up the Animal Spirit. When we die, our flesh rots and is consumed by the earth, to be again taken up by the Plant Spirits. With each cycle, our Spirits and the Wisdom they contain mixes further and further together, thus reinforcing our bond of unity on the Material Plane. If we could simply shed our preconceptions, then we would understand the wisdom that flows into us with each bite we eat. Unfortunately, many of us cannot do this, and do not even thank the spirits of those whom we have consumed. The Sacred Teacher Plants help us with this.

Shamans and the Sacred Teacher Plants

For the Shaman, there can be no practice without understanding of how to cultivate and prepare the Sacred Teacher Plants. The plants do not simply teach when consumed; their wisdom is also expressed to the Shaman through cultivation. For this reason, the Shaman absolutely must maintain a garden of as many of the Sacred Teacher Plants as possible, and develop skills in preparation and guiding others through rituals involving the consumption of preparations of these plants. Without these skills, one could not declare themselves to be a Shaman. This part of the religious practice structure is vastly more important than any training in energy manipulation or magic arts.

There are several different ritual settings in which the Sacred Teacher Plants are prepared and consumed, each with its own reason. Communing with the One involves sitting down with others and guiding them through the process of understanding their connection with all other things around them, and typically involves a Shaman working with a group of those whom he offers guidance and support to. The Vision Quest involves breaking free of the bonds of the Material Plane for a short time and traveling to the Spirit World in order to better understand the journey awaiting us in death and rebirth. Seeking the Oracle is a process of consuming and consulting with the Sacred Teacher Plants in order to find a better way to approach your problems. Finally, the last ritual described will be on Magical Empowerment, in which the Shaman consumes and consults with the Sacred Teacher Plants in order to find aid and better perception for working Magic Effects.

Without the Sacred Teacher Plants, a Shaman is incapable of seeing the truth behind our Material Plane. You cannot perform Communion without them. You will not be able to Vision Quest, seek an Oracle amongst the Spirits, or find empowerment through their Spirits for your Magic Practices. When you prepare your garden, keep in mind that the cultivation of these benevolent manifestations is a mirror of how much you care for yourself, and how you feel about all others around you. Use their growth as a source for joy, and thank them regularly for their contribution to you. In their material death, you will gain a source of spiritual life and insight. Respect them for this.

Communion

Communion is performed in order to celebrate and better understand your connection to all things around you, and the Unity of the One. Communions can be performed daily, weekly, or monthly, depending upon the circumstances; however, it should be performed at least once every other week. This frequency keeps it fresh in your mind that the idea of within and without are constructs of our perception, and do not exist in truth.

Indoors or outdoors, Communion can be performed pretty much wherever you are. Some take Communion as part of a large social event, such as a sports game, and others prefer to take it in a place more quiet, where they are surrounded by a veritable host of other plants and animals. The setting for your Communions should be a place where you will be comfortable and free from having to partake in any activity that could endanger the safety of yourself or others. Most Communions take place indoors, in a bedroom or living room of the house, with a few friends gathered together in a half-circle, all comfortably seated. Find what works best for you in the place you aim to Commune with the One.

Communions can be done solo or with a group. It all depends upon your needs and the availability of companions who follow a similar faith as yourself. If you take it alone, be certain that you won't be involving yourself in anything dangerous during the time the Sacred Teacher Plants are with you in strong experience, and that someone knows what you are doing. If you take it in a group, make certain that all issues concerning cooking, travel, or work are set aside until the experience is completed.

Start your Communion with the quote, out loud, "We are gathered here in this moment to transcend the self-imposed boundary of within and without, to see the Unity of the One, with the aid of the Sacred Teacher Plants." Say this with joy, and not with dire seriousness. This is a cause for celebration! Treat it as a joyful time, and not a time of concrete emotion. If you don't enter the Communion with a feeling of joyful bliss and happiness, then you aren't properly prepared for it.

After the quote, pass the preparation around to all who will consume it. Most communions use both a tea preparation or ground up portions of the plants in combination with other preparations for smoking. Pass the tea or the preparations to be eaten, and then pass the pipe after all have consumed. Make certain to thank the Spirits when you consume their bodies.

Once all have consumed their portions and the pipe is being passed around, a discussion on matters of meaning is engaged. This can range from simple daily activities to complex metaphysical discussions; it all depends on the group and what they are comfortable with. Speak freely with one another, for this encourages all to better feel the bond of unity between themselves.

Sometimes, the experience of the Sacred Teacher Plants in Communion becomes very strong, or some may feel the need to lay back and close their eyes. This is desirable, and as such a time for contemplation is usually set aside during the Communion. If some choose to speak during this time, it should be done quietly so as not to disturb those who are diving deeply within themselves and organizing their minds. Respect those who wish to simply sit back and allow the experience with the Plants to carry them away. If they choose to sleep, so be it. Let them rest.

Always enjoy the experience of Communion freely, and allow others to do the same. If you feel like dancing, singing, playing music, or anything that won't endanger yourself or another, do it! Communion is a time for joy and unity. The Spirits will respect you more if you don't hold back for fear of the opinions of others during this time. After all, enjoying the experience is the only way you will feel the One, and this is the entire purpose of engaging in Communion!

Vision Quest

The purpose of seeking the Vision Quest is to travel into the world beyond the Material. This is where the Spirits reside, from whence we came and to whence we return. Some seek the Vision Quest to better understand death, and therefore life; others seek it to find out which Spirits have elected themselves as guardian for them. Vision Quests are very serious matters, as they usually involve very strong experiences with the Sacred Plants, and a very deep dive within the organization of our own perceptions.

The Vision Quest can be taken indoors or outdoors, but a comfortable place to sit or lie down must be had, in a place where one will remain relatively undisturbed. Most find that the best place to have a Vision Quest is in a relatively wooded area that has been cleared to allow for comfort of a place to rest and a small fire to be built. Others prefer the comfort of their own homes. Whichever you decide is the best place for you, you must be absolutely comfortable and secure there.

The Vision Quest journey is always taken alone. This does not mean that others are not there with your Material Manifestation; it means that others cannot travel with you to the same place you are going. Vision Quests are always tailored to the needs of the individual within the experience. Often, a few people at a time will seek Vision Quests, and several others will engage in Communion while they watch over those on the Quest, warding away any energies that could prove harmful to those on the Quest, and prepared to help them back into their Material Manifestations and into the moment when they return. If you are on the Quest, trust in the Watchers. If you are a Watcher, be prepared to offer all the support you can to the person on the Quest, should they need it. Having two Watchers to each person Questing is the most optimal condition.

Begin the Vision Quest by stating, "I enter as though dead, to travel through the realms beyond Material, and am reborn through the journey." After this is stated, consume the preparations you have selected for this event. When you go on a Vision Quest, you should have something specific in mind you want to bring back with you from the journey. State this to your Watchers after you have consumed the preparations, and then lay back and relax, and wait for the experience to consume you.

Many people find it helpful to talk about what they see during the journey. This will help you return to your body in the end, and it will also help because we often forget all that we have experienced. Speaking about our visions allows the Watchers to know where you are, and will help them remind you later on of what you were seeing. The Watchers should not talk to you, except to ask you if you are comfortable and if you feel everything is going ok. If the experience is getting really rough and you're having trouble handling it, tell the Watchers and ask them to help you talk yourself back to the moment.

After you feel you have retrieved what you needed and the journey is complete, celebrate the experience with the Watchers. Dance, sing, or just talk to them. If others are still on their Quest, remember not to disturb them. Celebrate the Vision Quest, with great joy; you were just born again! If you are disturbed at the end and incapable of finding joy in the experience, then you were not adequately prepared. Always remember to clear away your troubles before Questing.

Consulting the Oracle

The Oracle is consulted during troubling times in your life. It should be only be consulted when you are confronted with a problem you have found that you are unable to view in any other way. This can concern finances, health, or romantic issues. Keep in mind that the purpose of consulting the Oracle is not to come away with information you couldn't acquire through other means; the purpose is to change your perspective to find a better way to deal with your problem.

Consulting the Oracle can be performed indoors or outdoors. A comfortable place to sit, quiet and free of distractions, will be all that is needed. Make certain that you won't be disturbed and you will feel completely safe in your setting.

Groups can perform this together, but each person who is Consulting the Oracle ultimately does it alone. During the consultation, you should not speak with others around you, and they should not speak with you. This will distract you from hearing the voice of the Spirits. It is possible for one person to act as Oracle, and have the others ask questions concerning their own issues. If this is the approach taken, then treat the person who is acting as Oracle as though they were a deity during the period of time they are the Oracle.

As you consume the preparation, speak aloud, "Sacred Teachers, unite with me as I consume you and help me to find better understanding of this problem." Seat yourself comfortably and speak aloud your problems to the Spirits. Then, quiet yourself and wait, with eyes open and fixed in the distant, for the messages from them. If you do not find them to be forthcoming, this is probably due to an insincerity on your part to face the problem, or an inability to relax and allow the Spirits to speak to you. On a very rare occasion, however, you will find no answer because there is none that can be given, and you need to face the problem as it is.

After your answers have been given, celebrate the occasion freely, and with joy! You must always find joy and celebration after each of these rituals; it is imperative if you are to show respect to the Spirits whose flesh you have just consumed. They will always come to you readily if you show great regard to them in this way.

Magical Empowerment

Using the Sacred Teacher Plants for Magical Empowerment requires submission to their wisdom. You must be completely receptive to their communications if you will ask help from them; they will not be able to assist you if you do not allow them this. Always request first off for sensitivity and perception, and then ask for their powers to be added to your own. You will find oftentimes that an increase in your own sensitivity will be all that is needed to work your Magic Effect.

Magical Empowerment can take place indoors or outdoors. The setting is really dependent upon what kind of a magic technique you will perform as part of this ritual. Always make certain that it is completely comfortable, and that the area has been prepared beforehand for magic workings.

Whether you do this alone or with a group is also dependent upon what kind of a magic technique you will employ. All who take part in the magic must take part in the Magical Empowerment Ritual, and the reverse is the same. If it is a group working, function wholly as a group. Also keep in mind that whether you have fellow humans working with you or not, there will be Spirits added to your group.

Begin the ritual by stating, "As we consume your body, help us to be more sensitive to the Ether and motivate it more effectively." Consume the preparations at this time, with total somberness. Place your mind upon the magic task ahead. While you wait for the experience to begin fully, practicing Five Gates Breath and Circulating the Aura. When the experience is fully upon you, then begin to work your Magic.

Once the Magic Effect has been performed, have an open celebration amongst the group. Play music, sing, dance, or just entertain yourselves in whatever way you feel is best. Remember to show joy and unconditional acceptance for all those around you; this will make the experience even greater for all involved.

Cultivation and Preparation

Contained herein are descriptions, cultivation and preparation techniques for 17 of the Sacred Teacher Plants. This list by no means contains all of the Sacred Teacher Plants; those listed here were selected for their ease of cultivation across a wide range of climates and gardening skill levels. It is up to you to inform yourself on not only all of the Sacred Teacher Plants known today, but also to research the plants listed here further from other sources. There are many techniques for growing and using these plants, and the more informed you are, the better consideration you will have for them. The beginner should have little problem using the information found herein to cultivate and use these Sacred Teacher Plants.

Argyria Nervosa "Baby Hawaiian Wood Rose"

Plant Description

Perennial climbing vine with large, heart-shaped leaves that may reach 1' in length and 8" in width, back with silvery hairs. Flowers are 2-3" long, magenta colored, and appear on 6" stalks. Flowers are succeeded by seed pods that darken with maturity and contain several large, bean-shaped brown seeds with a fuzzy outer coating.

Native Habitat

Tropical and sub-tropical regions from India across to the Polynesian Islands.

Preferred Growth Conditions

Prefers fertile, free-draining neutral to slightly acidic loam in full sun with frequent watering and high humidity. Grows best in temperatures between 65-95 degrees F. Frost tender, drought tolerant.

Propagation

Propagates by seed. Nick seeds slightly with a sharp knife away from the germ-eye and soak in room temperature water for two hours before sowing in a seed tray with moist soil. Just cover seeds with soil. Keep the soil moist, but not damp, as seeds and seedlings are susceptible to fungal rot. Seeds germinate within 7-21 days. Transplant seedlings after six leaves have sprouted. Seeds and seedlings can be left in full sun, as long as the soil does not dry out.

Cultivation

Argyria Nervosa does well planted in the ground or potted, but it must be protected from temperatures below 40 degrees F. Keep the soil moist, and the plant in full sun. Fertilize with a balanced blend (7-7-7) every other week. In its first year, this plant will resemble a small shrub. In its second year, it will begin to climb and produce flowers. Provide support for the vines when they begin to climb with a trellis or other implement.

Harvest

Seed pods are harvested after completely drying on the plant. Keep harvested pods in a dry, cool location away from direct sunlight, preferably stored in an air-tight container.

Preparation

8-10 seeds per person are removed from the pods, and the empty pods discarded. The fuzzy outer covering of the seeds is then scraped off, and the seeds crushed for consumption. The onset of the experience is usually 45 to 60 minutes after ingestion, and lasts for 6 to 8 hours. This experience is characterized by a slight lethargy, euphoria, visions, and sleeplessness.

Diet Restrictions

Consult your physician before you consume this plant preparation if you are or may become pregnant, are nursing, or if you suffer from any chronic medical condition or are currently prescribed any medications. Observe a six-hour fast before consuming this preparation. Do not combine with Ipomoea Violacea preparation.

Banisteriopsis Caapi "Ayahuasca Vine"

Plant Description

Woody perennial climbing vine with green, oval-shaped leaves which range in size from 3 to 7 inches long and 1 to 4 inches wide. B. Caapi rarely flowers.

Native Habitat

Found in the tropical rainforests of the Amazon in South America.

Preferred Growth Conditions

Prefers fertile, free-draining, moist acidic sandy loam positioned in part sun. Soil must remain moist at all times; this plant is very drought sensitive. Frost resistant to 25 degrees F. Must have climbing support to grow well.

Propagation

Propagates by cuttings, due to the rarity of flowering. Take a cutting by removing the top 6 inches of new growth. Strip the lower 3 inches of leaves and dust with a rooting agent. Place in moist soil, with the lowest leaf just above the surface of the soil. Keep the cutting out of direct sunlight, but in bright light, and maintain at 90% humidity between 65 and 75 degrees F. Cutting will begin to root in 7-14 days. Transplant after new growth appears.

Cultivation

Banisteriopsis Caapi can be maintained in pots, but it prefers to be planted out so its root structure can fully develop. If pots are used, they must be 25 gallon sized or larger. Water frequently enough to keep the soil moist, but not saturated. Lightly fertilize with a balanced blend (7-7-7) once a week. This plant absolutely must have climbing support available if it is to grow. Keep in part shade. If properly cared for, this plant will produce nearly 1 foot of growth per day during the spring and summer.

Harvest

1 foot sections ¾ to 1 inch thick are removed at the end of the growth season. Care must be taken not to remove the lowest 3 feet of the vine, or it may be killed. Preserve removed portions of vine by drying and storing in a cool, dry area out of direct sunlight.

Preparation

1 foot of vine per person is pounded until the vine is broken down into a fibrous mass, then boiled at a low temperature in slightly acidic water for six hours. The water is then strained off and consumed. This liquid is often combined with the preparations of D. Illinoensis, P. Arundinacae, P. Cubensis, or P. Viridis. The experience is usually first felt 30 minutes after ingestion, and is characterized by drowsiness, relaxation, and closed-eye visions, typically lasting between four and six hours.

Diet Restrictions

Consult your physician before you consume this plant preparation if you are or may become pregnant, are nursing, or if you suffer from any chronic medical condition or are currently taking any medications.

This plant preparation contains several Mono-Amine Oxidase Inhibitors known as Beta-Carbolines. MAO is an enzyme in the stomach that prevents potentially toxic chemicals from being digested and absorbed into the blood stream. When this enzyme is blocked, normally harmless foods including some fruits and vegetables can be potentially fatal. For safety, consume no food other than boiled rice, citrus fruit and juices, and roasted fresh fish for 2 days before and after consuming this plant preparation. Do not consume any fermented foods or beverages during this time. Observe a minimum of a 10-hour fast before consuming B. Caapi preparation.

Cannabis Sativa "Indian Hemp"

Description

Herbaceous annual with erect stems and dark green, serrated edge, palmate leaves with 5 to 7 leaflets. C. Sativa grows from 3 to 10 feet in height, and at times even taller. Flowers are unisexual; male flowers have 5 almost separate downy segments, and the female a single hairy leaf which encloses the ovary in a sheath. The fruit produced is a small, oval black seed and can account for over half the weight of the entire plant in maturity.

Native Habitat

This plant has been cultivated worldwide for fiber for so long that its original origin is unknown. Found nearly everywhere save the polar regions.

Preferred Growth Conditions

Prefers fertile, free-draining, well aerated acidic sandy loam in full sun to part shade with frequent watering. Frost tender to 25 degrees F, drought resistant.

Propagation

Propagates well by seed or cuttings. Seeds should be sown in seed trays, just covered with soil, and kept in bright light. Keep the soil moist but not saturated. Seeds germinate in 3 to 7 days. Seedlings can be transplanted when they reach 4 or 5 inches tall.

Cuttings should be taken by removing the top 6 inches of the plant or branch tip, dusted with rooting agent, and burying the lower 3 inches in moist soil. Keep cuttings out of direct sunlight, but in bright light. Cuttings should root within 7 to 14 days.

Transplant when new growth appears. Do not plant out seedlings or cuttings to be sown into the ground until all danger of frost has passed.

Cultivation

Grows well in 5 to 8 gallon pots or in the ground. If potted, the pots should be at least 5 gallon sized. When planting in the ground, space the plants 6 inches apart in rows 3 feet apart. Water regularly enough to keep the soil moist. Fertilize once a week with a balanced blend (7-7-7) or brands advertised for tomatoes. Keep the plants in full sun to part shade. Flowers will appear typically between 6-10 weeks after germination; unless much seed is required, male plants should be culled as soon as they are identified as such.

Harvest

80-100 days after germination, when the seeds have begun to ripen on the plant, the entire plant is harvest by slicing the stalk just above ground level. Strip the flowers and foliage and store in a brown paper bag in a dry, dark spot for approximately two weeks for drying. After they have dried completely, store in airtight containers or bags. Shelf life is about one year.

Preparation

Seeds and stems are cleared away from the flowering parts, and the buds are broken down into very small pieces. About 1 gram of the flowering material is smoked per person. Seeds are saved for replanting, and the stems are discarded. Alternately, 10 grams of dry foliage per person can be combined with 1 cup of hot water and steeped for 30 minutes, and the water then strained off and consumed. Onset of experience for smoking is immediate, for tea is 20 to 30 minutes, and both typically last 4 to 6 hours. Effects including euphoria, drowsiness, relaxation, and lethargy.

Diet Restrictions

Consult your physician before you consume this plant preparation if you are or may become pregnant, are nursing, or if you suffer from any chronic medical condition or are currently prescribed any medications.

This plant preparation is considered to be a compliment to any other plant preparations listed herein.

Desmanthus Illinoensis "Prairie Mimosa"

Description

Herbaceous perennial with green, alternate, doubly pinnate leaves which grows to a height of 5 to 7 feet tall. Flowering parts are greenish-white, and are so small that they cannot be distinguished by the naked eye. The fruit is a tight cluster of highly twisted seed pods in which 2 to 5 brown seeds may be found.

Native Habitat

Found in North America, from the southeast to the Great Lakes and spreading across the Midwest.

Preferred Growth Conditions

Prefers fertile, free draining acidic soils with lots of sun and moisture. D. Illinoensis grows readily in light and heavy soils, and can manage in nutrient-poor ground due to the nitrogen fixers in its roots. Free draining, enriched soil in full sun will produce the best growth. This plant is cold hard to –30 degrees F, but is only moderately drought resistant.

Propagation

Propagates by seed. Seeds can be sown directly into the ground, spaced 1 foot apart in rows spaced to 3 feet, in the spring after all danger of frost has passed. Alternately, they may be sown in moist soil in seed trays and planted out when they reach 4 to 6 inches tall. Seeds germinate in 14-21 days. Place seed trays in direct sunlight, and keep the soil moist but not saturated.

Cultivation

Desmanthus Illinoensis must be planted in the ground in full sun, it does not grow well in pots. Only water established plants if the ground is no longer moist ¼ inch below the surface, or during prolonged periods without rain. Fertilize every two weeks during the spring and summer with a balanced blend (7-7-7) to accelerate growth.

Harvest

After three full seasons of growth, the plant is lifted up out of the ground and the roots removed. The roots may be completely harvested and the remainder of the plant composted, or the roots may be lightly pruned and the shrub replanted. This is best performed in late fall to early winter, especially if it will be replanted, for this reduces shock to the plant and is the most potent time of harvest. The harvested roots are then washed thoroughly to remove all dirt and pounded until the root bark separates from the core. The root bark is then dried, with the core discarded. Store root bark in a cool, dark location in moisture and air proof containers.

Preparation

20 to 25 grams root bark per person is ground and boiled for 4 hours in 2 cups of slightly acidified water. The water is then strained off and consumed in combination with B. Caapi or P. Harmala preparations. The onset of the experience occurs typically within 30 to 45 minutes after ingestion and last 4 to 6 hours. Effects includes open and closed eye visions, heightened perceptions, euphoria, and sleeplessness.

Diet Restrictions

Consult your physician before you consume this plant preparation if you are or may become pregnant, are nursing, or if you suffer from any chronic medical condition or are currently prescribed any medications.

This preparation must be consumed with B. Caapi or P. Harmala preparations to be effective. Read and follow the diet restriction guidelines for those plants before you consume this preparation.

Ephedra Major "Ma Huang"

Description

Perennial succulent with leathery leaves reaching 1 inch in length and 1/8 to ¼ inch in width. Mature plants can reach up to 6 feet in height and 4 feet in width. Male and female flowers appear on different plants, and each sex must be grown if seeds are to be acquired. Flowers are white or yellow, and are followed by fruit which appears as red or yellow globes and usually contains 6-9 seeds.

Native Habitat

Native from the Mediterranean region and West Asia to the Himalayas.

Preferred Growth Conditions

Prefers fertile, loose, free-draining soil in full sun. Soil must be either dry or just moist, and not damp or soggy. Grows well in any pH type. Will not grow in shade; must be maintained in full sun. Frost hard to –5 degree F, very drought tolerant.

Propagation

Propagates by seed. Sow seed in moist soil in seed trays placed in full sun, just covering seeds with soil. Seeds germinate in 3 to 7 days. Keep soil barely moistened by misting for germination and seedlings, and allow it to dry completely on the surface before re-misting. Transplant when seedlings reach 4 inches or more in height, taking care not to damage the root structure.

Cultivation

Ephedra Major does well in 3 gallon pots and in the ground in appropriate climates. It should only be watered just enough to keep the ground slightly moist. Allow the soil to dry out between watering. Keep plants in full sun at all times. Fertilize once a month during the spring and summer with a balanced blend (7-7-7.) Plants should be protected during the winter of their first year. After the first year, they may be left outside as long as temperatures do not fall below 0 degrees F. If the plant dies back to its roots during the winter, it will typically recover during the following spring.

Harvest

Branches may be removed from well established plants when it reaches between 2 and 3 feet in height. Preserve these by drying, then shred the plant material and store in a cool, dark place in air and moisture proof containers. Seeds are harvested when the fruit dries completely on the plant, or begins to fall off.

Preparation

3 grams of shredded material per person is steeped in 1 cup boiling water for 20 minutes. The water is then strained off and consumed. The onset of the experience is typically within 10 to 30 minutes after ingestion and last 3 to 4 hours. Effects include euphoria, heightened perceptions, alertness, restlessness, and sleeplessness.

Diet Restrictions

Consult your physician before you consume this plant preparation if you are or may become pregnant, are nursing, or if you suffer from any chronic medical condition or are currently prescribed medications.

Do not combine this plant preparation with any Mono-Amine Oxidase Inhibitors. B. Caapi and P. Harmala both contain several Beta-Carboline class MAOI's, and should not be used in conjunction with this plant preparation.

Erythroxylum Coca "Coca Bush"

Description

Evergreen perennial shrub with dark green oval or elliptical leaves which grow from 4 to 6 inches long and 2 to 4 inches wide. Can reach heights of up to 18 feet, with the root system penetrating 20 feet or more into the soil. Almond scented flowers can be white or yellow and are succeeded by red berries containing only one seed each.

Native Habitat

Grows from Mexico south to Peru, and can be found in the West Indies.

Preferred Growth Conditions

Prefers fertile, free draining, acidic sandy loam in full to part sun with high humidity. Does not tolerate drought. Frost hardy to 25 degree F.

Propagation

Propagates by seed or cuttings. Seeds remain viable for only 3 to 4 weeks after maturing, and should be sown within 1 week of maturity. Soak seeds for 6 hours in water, then sow in seed trays, just covering with moist soil. Soil should be kept moist, but not damp. Seeds germinate in 20-35 days if kept between 75 and 85 degrees F at high humidity. Seedlings can be planted out when they reach 4 to 6 inches in height.

Cuttings can be taken by removing an 18 inch branch tip, preparing the lower 12 inches with rooting agent, and burying the prepared portion completely in moist soil. Cutting will root fully within 6 to 8 weeks. Viable seeds cannot be obtained from a cutting.

Cultivation

Erythroxylum Coca cannot be easily cultivated in pots unless a bonsai technique is used due to their extensive root structure. Maintain in 5 gallon, wide pots, and trim the roots once a month to keep them trained back. Do not allow a bush maintained in a pot to exceed 2.5 feet high, or 2 feet wide. If it will be planted outside, space bushes to 4 feet on all sides. Maintain in full sun. Water frequently enough to keep the soil moist at all times. Fertilize once a week in the spring and summer with a balanced blend (7-7-7.) Protect from frost.

Harvest

Leaves are removed from 2 year old bushes and dried quickly to prevent fermentation. Take care not to remove more than 1/3 of the plant's foliage during a harvest, and allow ample opportunity for the plant to replenish its leaves before re-harvesting. Dried leaves should be stored in a cool, dark location in air and moisture free containers.

Preparations

20 grams of foliage per person are chewed for 30 minutes, with the juices swallowed and the pulp discarded. Alternately, the same quantity may be covered with water and boiled at a low temperature for 1 hour, with the water then strained off and consumed. The onset of the experience usually begins with 20 minutes of chewing or drinking the tea and lasts for 1 to 2 hours. Effects include mild numbness of the mouth, throat, and stomach, euphoria, relaxation, and mild analgesia.

Diet Restrictions

Consult your physician before you consume this plant preparation if you are or may become pregnant, are nursing, or if you suffer from any chronic medical condition or are currently prescribed any medications. This plant preparation is considered to be highly nutritive, and is a compliment to any other plant preparations listed herein.

Ipomoea Violacea "Tri-Color Morning Glory"

Description

Perennial twining vine which grows 10 to 20 feet long. Leaves are heart-shaped and grow to 5 inches long and up to 3 inches wide. Flowers are funnel shaped and range in color from blue, red, to white, with white throats on the blue and red varieties. Fruit is small green pods containing 5 to 9 seeds which darken to a near-black color when the seeds reach maturity.

Native Habitat

Native from the southernmost parts of North America through Central America and South America.

Preferred Growth Conditions

Prefers fertile, free-draining acidic sandy loam in full to part sun, with plenty of moisture. Frost sensitive, drought tolerant. Grows best when provided with climbing support.

Propagation

Propagates by seed. Sow seeds 6 inches apart in the ground after danger of frost has passed, or in a seed tray, just covering with soil. Seeds germinate in 7 to 14 days. Seedlings can be transplanted when they reach 4 inches in height

Cultivation

Grows well in 2 to 5 gallon pots or in the ground. Keep in full to part sun and provide climbing support. Water frequently, but do not allow the soil to become saturated. Fertilize with a flowering formula (7-14-7 or similar) once a week in the spring and summer. Ipomoea Violacea can be cultivated as an annual, due to its frequent flowering. Flowers 6 to 8 weeks after germination. Protect from frost during the winter if you wish to maintain it as a perennial. If not, replant seeds each spring.

Harvest

Seeds are harvested after the pods have completely darkened and dried on the vine. Remove seeds from the pods and discard pod material. Store seeds in a cool, dark location in air and moisture free containers.

Preparation

12 grams of seeds per person are crushed and consumed. Alternately, the same quantity may be crushed and soaked in cold water for six hours, with the water then strained off and consumed. Onset of experience begins in 45 to 60 minutes after ingestion and lasts for 6 to 8 hours. Effects include open and closed eye visions, restlessness, sleeplessness, enhanced perceptions, euphoria, and drowsiness.

Diet Restrictions

Consult your physician before you consume this plant preparation if you are or may become pregnant, are nursing, or if you suffer from any chronic medical condition or are currently prescribed any medications.

Do not combine with Argyria Nervosa preparation. Observe a 6 to 8 hour fast before consuming this plant preparation.

Lophophora Williamsii "Peyote"

Description

Spineless, tufted, slow-growing blue-green cactus which resembles a button on the top and has a 6 inch long root which resembles a carrot. Flowers appear amidst a wooly center on the top of the button after 5 to 8 years growth, and produce many small black seeds.

Native Habitat

Southern Texas and Northern Mexico near the Rio Grande.

Preferred Growth Conditions

Prefers fertile, free-draining, calcium-rich alkaline sandy loam in an arid location. Does not grow well in direct sunlight, due to a tendency to burn easily. Always found in the wild under the shade of bushes, where it receives filtered sunlight. Highly drought tolerant, frost resistant to 29 degrees F.

Propagation

Propagates by seed or cutting. Seeds should be sown in trays and just covered with moist soil. Keep the soil just slightly moist by misting, and maintain in a high humidity environment between 70 and 80 degrees F. Seeds will germinate in 7 to 21 days. Maintain in bright, but not direct sunlight. Seedlings can be transplanted when the button tops reach ½ inch in diameter; care must be taken not to damage the root structure when transplanting.

Cuttings can be taken from mature plants by gently removing just the button from the root with a sterilized knife, after the button has reached 2 inches in diameter. The button must be sliced away at least 1/8 inch above the soil line so the root remains undamaged and can produce several new buttons. The wound on the removed portion is allowed several days to completely callous over. After callusing, it is placed wound-down on dry, loose soil. New roots will form in 2 to 3 months. During this time, the button may be lightly misted occasionally to help it receive moisture. Do not water the soil until new roots have been established.

Cultivation

Lophophora Williamsii grows well in 2 or 3 gallon pots which are deep enough to allow the root structure to grow unimpeded. Keep out of direct sunlight. A shading cloth may be used to achieve this. Water just enough to keep the soil moist in the spring and summer. Do not water in the fall or winter. Lightly fertilize monthly with a balanced blend (7-7-7) or a blend especially marketed for cacti. Protect from frost in the winter. The growth of this cactus is extremely slow. It may take 5 years of growth for the button to reach 3 inches in diameter, and up to 10 for it to reach flowering maturity.

Harvest

The button tops of Lophophora Williamsii may be harvested after they have flowered and produced seed. This may take between 5 and 15 years of growth, depending upon conditions. Remove the button by gently cleaning the dirt from around the plant and cutting just above the root. Several new buttons will appear if the root structure remains undamaged. Buttons can be preserved by drying and storing in a cool, dark location in air and moisture-proof containers.

Preparation

20 grams dried buttons per person are chewed, with the juices swallowed. Alternately, the some quantity may be boiled in acidified water a very low temperature

for 3 to 4 hours, with the water strained off and consumed. Onset of the experience occurs in 45 to 90 minutes, and typically lasts 6 to 10 hours. Effects included open and closed eye visions, euphoria, a sense of an increase in body temperature and perspiration, sleeplessness, and quietude.

Diet Restrictions

Consult your physician before you consume this plant preparation if you are or may become pregnant, are nursing, or if you suffer from any chronic medical condition or are currently prescribed any medications.

Do not combine this plant preparation with any Mono-Amine Oxidase Inhibitors. B. Caapi and P. Harmala both contain several Beta-Carboline class MAOI's, and should not be used in conjunction with this plant preparation.

Do not combine with Trichocereus Pachanoi preparation. Observe a 10 to 12 hour fast before consuming this plant preparation.

Nicotiana Rustica "Turkish Tobacco"

Description

Herbaceous annual which reaches 3 to 6 feet in height. Leaves are pale-green, somewhat oval, and can grow to 1 foot in length and width. Flowers are yellow-green, and are followed by smallish pods which contain many miniscule, dark-brown seeds.

Native Habitat

North, Central, and South America. Now cultivated worldwide.

Preferred Growth Conditions

Prefers, fertile, free-draining sandy loam in full sun. Grows well in nearly any soil condition or pH. Established plants are drought resistant. Frost tender at 32 degrees F.

Propagation

Propagates by seed. Seeds can be sown in the ground after all danger of frost has passed, or started in seed trays and just covered with moist soil. Seed trays should be left in full sun, and the soil kept just moistened. Seedlings may be transplanted or thinned out when they reach 2 to 3 inches tall.

Cultivation

Nicotiana Rustica can be grown in 5 gallon pots, but it does best when planted out in the ground. Space plants to 1 foot, and rows at 3 feet apart. Water frequently enough to keep the soil moist. Fertilize once a week during the growing season with a balanced blend (7-7-7.) This plant is a severe soil depleter; the ground must be heavily fertilized after each season of growth.

Harvest

Leaves are removed from the stems and allowed to dry during the second week of fall. Dried leaves should be stored in a cool, dark place in air and moisture free containers.

Preparation

Dry leaves are shredded, with 1 gram material per person smoked. Alternately, whole leaves may be used to roll up quantities of C. Sativa, N. Rustica, and P. Somniferum preparations mixed together to form cigars. The onset of the experience is immediate, and lasts for 20 to 60 minutes. Effects include dizziness, euphoria, increased vitality and vigor, and relaxation.

Diet Restrictions

Consult your physician before you consume this plant preparation if you are or may become pregnant, are nursing, or if you suffer from any chronic medical condition or are currently prescribed any medication.

Nicotiana Rustica is considered to be a compliment to any other plant preparation listed herein.

Papaver Somniferum "Opium Poppy"

Description

Herbaceous annual or biannual with an erect stem which grows from 1.5 to 3 feet tall. Leaves are numerous, erect, oval to oblong shaped with serrated edges and grow from 4 to 7 inches long and 2 to 4 inches wide. Flowers appear on long peduncles with nodding buds which expand into erect flowers. Fruit is globe shaped, green seed pods full of many gray, black, white, or bluish oily seeds. Petals drop 5 to 9 days after flowering, leaving the bulbous green seed pods on top of the stalks.

Native Habitat

Native from the Mediterranean west across Asia to the Malay Peninsula.

Preferred Growth Conditions

Prefers fertile, moist, acidic sandy loam in full sun in tropical and sub tropical climates. Established plants are drought resistant. Frost tender at 32 degrees F.

Propagation

Propagates by seed. Seeds can be sown in trays and just covered in moist soil, or planted out in the ground spaced 6 inches apart in rows 3 feet apart. Seedlings can be transplanted or thinned out when they reach 3 inches tall. Seeds germinate in 3 to 7 days. Keep trays in full sunlight, and do not allow the soil to dry out.

Cultivation

Grows well in 3 to 5 gallon pots or in the ground. Keep in full sun. Water frequently enough to keep the ground moist, but not saturated. Fertilize every two weeks with a balanced blend (7-7-7) in the spring and summer. Flowers appear within 6 to 8 weeks after germination.

Harvest

5 to 7 days after the petals drop from the pods, the pods are lightly scratched with a razor blade or a pin in three horizontal strokes on one side, with care taken not to pierce the pod. The sap is allowed to leech out of these wounds and dry, and is then scraped off a few hours later with a dull knife. After waiting a day, the process is repeated on the opposite side of the seed pod. 33 to 35 days after the petals drop, the pods are removed from the stem and allowed to dry completely. Preserve sap and pods by thoroughly drying and storing in a cool, dry location in moisture free containers.

Preparation

½ gram sap per person is smoked or ingested. Alternately, 2 seed pods per person are sliced open, the seeds removed, and the pods then boiled in 1 or 2 cups of water for 30 minutes. This water is then strained off and consumed. Onset of experience for smoking is immediate and lasts for 4 to 6 hours. Onset of experience for seed pod tea is 20 to 30 minutes, and lasts 4 to 6 hours. Effects include light nausea, euphoria, lightheadedness, relaxation, sedation, moderate pain relief or numbness of extremities, closed eye visions, and lethargy.

Diet Restrictions

Consult your physician before consuming this plant preparation if you are or may become pregnant, are nursing, or if you suffer from any chronic medical condition or are currently prescribed any medications.

Do not combine this plant preparation with any Mono-Amine Oxidase Inhibitors. B. Caapi and P. Harmala preparations both contain several Beta-Carboline class MAOI's, and should not be used in conjunction with this plant preparation.

Peganum Harmala "Syrian Rue"

Description

Herbaceous perennial succulent which grows to about 4 feet tall and 2 to 3 feet wide. Leaves are bright green, deeply pinnatifid, and grow to about 2 inches long and 1 inch at the widest. Flowers are white with 5 petals, and occur singly along the stem at leaf forks. Flowers are succeeded by spherical, 3-valved fruit which ranges from ¼ to ¾ inch in diameter. Fruit turns from green to a brownish orange when ripe, and opens at the top of the valves.

Native Habitat

Native to the arid regions of North Africa, the Mediterranean, the Middle East, and across to India and Pakistan.

Preferred Growth Conditions

Prefers fertile, free-draining, well-aerated sandy loam in full sun. Peganum Harmala is highly drought tolerant and prefers infrequent water. Frost hardy to 10 degrees F; sometimes dies back to its roots during the winter, but will rapidly re-grow in the spring unless the root ball freezes.

Propagation

Propagates by seed. Sow seed in seed trays and just cover with moist soil. Keep soil moist by misting, and maintain in full sun. Seeds will germinate in 3 to 10 days. Seedlings may be transplanted when they reach 3 or 4 inches in height.

Cultivation

Grows well in 3 to 5 gallon pots. Keep in full sun. Water only when top ¼ inch of soil is no longer moist. Fertilize every two weeks in the spring and summer with a balanced blend (7-7-7.) Protect plants from frost during their first winter. Plants produce seed in their second or third year.

Harvest

Seeds are harvested from the pods after the pods change color and open at the valves. Clear pods away from seed, and store seeds in a cool, dark location in air and moisture free containers.

Preparation

5 grams seed per person are crushed and ingest. Onset of experience is 15 to 30 minutes, and it generally lasts 4 to 6 hours. Effects include open and closed eye visions, euphoria, elevated mood, drowsiness, and nausea.

Diet Restrictions

Consult your physician before you consume this plant preparation if you are or may become pregnant or are nursing, or if you suffer from any chronic medical condition or are currently prescribed any medications.

This plant preparation contains several MAOI's known as Beta-Carbolines. Mono-Amine Oxidase is an enzyme in the stomach that prevents potentially toxic chemicals from being digested and absorbed into the blood stream. When this enzyme is blocked, normally harmless foods including some fruits and vegetables can be potentially fatal. For safety, consume no food other than boiled rice, citrus fruit and juices, and roasted fresh fish for 2 days before and after consuming this plant preparation. Do not consume any fermented foods or beverages during this time.

Phalaris Arundinacae "Gardener's Garters"

Description

Invasive perennial grass which grows to heights of 4 to 5 feet. Leaves are green on most varieties and hairless; however, var. Tricolor is variegated, with yellow stripes which tint red in the spring and fall. Spreads aggressively by creeping rhizomes. New shoots contain a noticeable red tinge. Flowers appear in the late summer in yellow spikes, and are follow by clusters of husk-covered black seeds.

Native Habitat

North and Southeastern North America, spreading across to the Mississippi river. Cultivated across North America as cattle fodder.

Preferred Growth Conditions

Prefers fertile, moist, acidic sandy loam in full sun. Tolerant of drought and flood conditions. Frost resistant to –15 degrees F.

Propagation

Propagates by seed. Sow seed in moist soil in pots or in the ground, scattering them across the surface of the soil. Keep moist by lightly watering, and maintain in full sun. Seeds germinate in 3 to 10 days. Transplant by moving entire sections of seedlings and soil to desired cultivation area.

Cultivation

Grows well in pots of any size or the ground. Keep in full sun, as this plant does not tolerate shade well. Water frequently. Fertilize weekly with a balanced blend (7-7-7) in spring, summer and fall. Pruning regularly greatly stimulates growth.

Harvest

Leaves and stems are harvested by pruning back to an even 6 inch height. Preserve by thoroughly drying clippings and storing in a cool, dark location in air and moisture free containers.

Preparation

100 to 150 grams dried clippings per person are covered in acidified water and boiled for 6 hours. The water is then strained off and consumed. Must be combined with B. Caapi or P. Harmala preparations. Onset of experience is usually 30 to 60 minutes after ingestion, and typically lasts 4 to 6 hours. Effects include euphoria, restlessness, nausea, open and closed eye visions, and drowsiness.

Diet Restrictions

Consult your physician before you consume this plant preparation if you are or may become pregnant, are nursing, or if you suffer from any chronic medical condition or are currently prescribed any medications. This preparation must be consumed with B. Caapi or P. Harmala preparations to be effective. Read and follow the diet restriction guidelines for those plants before you consume this preparation.

Psilocybe Cubensis "Magic Mushrooms"

Description

Mushroom with yellow to golden brown cap which measures from ¾ to 4 inches broad, often spotted with remnants of the universal veil. The stem is whitish, sometimes discoloring to yellow, and ranges in height from 2 to 9 inches. Gills are grayish in young carpophores, but turn blackish purple as it matures and spores are produced. Spores are a dark purplish black. Mycelium is white, with a fibrous quality. All parts readily bruise blue.

Native Habitat

Found worldwide in tropical and subtropical regions, and in many temperate zones during the spring and summer.

Preferred Growth Conditions

Found in the wild upon the manure of many herbivores and on heavily manured ground during the warm seasons when the temperature ranges between 60 and 90 degrees F. Prefers high humidity and adequate moisture, though rains will down growth. Does not tolerate temperatures below 45 degrees F. Can be readily cultivated on most grains if attention to moisture, humidity, and temperature are maintained.

Propagation

Propagates by spores. Spores are hydrated in sterile distilled water and allowed to sit for 48 hours. This spore solution is then drawn up into a sterilize syringe and injected into jars containing growth medium. Growth medium is prepared by grinding ¼ cup brown rice and combining it with ½ cup fine particle vermiculite and ½ cup water per jar. Water content should be adjusted so that the medium is able to hold a shape if pressed together, but not soggy. This growth medium, also called substrate, is then packed lightly into wide mouth half pint canning jars up to the bottom thread. The rest of the space in the jar is then filled with additional dry vermiculite.

If two piece canning lids are used, the rubber seal is left upwards and band lightly screwed on. If one piece canning lids are used, do not seal the lid tightly. The lid is further prepared by drilling 4 equal distance holes on the edge as close to the band as possible with a 1/8 inch drill bit. These holes are then covered with small squares of painting grade masking tape. Jars are then placed in a pressure cooker, and sterilized at 15 pounds pressure for 1 hour.

Allow the jars to cool completely before injecting ¼ cc of spore solution into each hole on the lid, making certain the needle is pushed all the way down to the growth medium, and the spore solution visibly runs down the glass side of the jar. Flame sterilize the needle tip before injecting any solution into the jars. White strands of mycelial growth, the root-like network and main body of the mushroom, will appear at the injection sites within 3 to 7 days. Take care to completely disinfect your working area and hands before injecting any solution into the jars.

Cultivation

Cultivating Psilocybe Cubensis to fruiting requires an environment with a controlled humidity between 90% and 95%, and a controlled temperature of no less than 65 degrees F and no greater than 80 degrees F. It also requires bright light, but not direct sunlight. This is best achieved by constructing an airtight terrarium with a clear lid. Many 66 quart storage containers can be slightly modified to fit this task. Humidity can be provided by drilling a hole in lower part of the side of the container large enough for an aquarium air hose to fit through and running a line in from a small aquarium air pump. A bubble stone is attached to the line in the terrarium and placed in a 20 ounce soda bottle half-full of water. The line should be secured to the mouth of the bottle so the bubble stone remains at the bottom. If humidity drops, it can be raised by lightly misting water from a spray bottle into the terrarium. Humidity and temperature can be monitored by affixing a small digital gauge to the inside of the terrarium. Light can be provided by a fluorescent aquarium fixture set on top of the container and timed to a 12 hour cycle per day. The inside of the terrarium must be cleansed with disinfectant prior to use, and should any water accumulate in the bottom at any time, it must be immediately wiped out.

5 days after the mycelium has completely covered the substrate in the jars, the jars should be turned upside down so the cakes slide downwards. The jar may need to be lightly tapped to free the mycelium which clings to the glass. Turn the jar right-side up again after the cake has been freed and remove the lid. Cover the jar mouth with a small tray, and invert the jar again so the substrate cake slides down onto the tray. Immediately place the tray and cake within the terrarium. Within 3 to 14 days after moving the cakes to the terrarium, tiny white pin-like structures will appear. These will grow into full size fruiting bodies with 7 to 10 days.

To ensure continued fruiting, it is necessary to provide the mycelium with an adequate supply of water. This can be accomplished by adding 3 to 4 droplets of water to the vermiculite layer beneath the cake every few days. This lay should remain slightly moist, but never soggy. Wipe away any excess water droplets with the corner of a paper towel.

If the cake begins to turn blue, this is due to lack of moisture and it needs to be top-cased. Top-casing involves mixing vermiculite with enough water to just moisten it, and then adding a ¼ to ½ inch thick layer to the top of the cake. Water may be added to this in a few droplets at a time, to maintain a low level of moisture. Cakes will produce mushrooms for 3 to 4 months if kept properly hydrated. If at any time during the cycle the cake appears to grow any mold or bacteria, which are typically evidenced by browns, greens, or orange colors, discard immediately. These growths can be very harmful if consumed, and will destroy any other cakes which are left in the terrarium along side it.

Harvest

Carpophores, the fruiting body, are removed with a sharp knife or scissors by cutting the base of the stem away from the substrate cake. If no spores are desired, harvest the fruiting body as soon as the universal veil which covers the gills tears away from the stem. If you wish to harvest spores along with the fruiting body, you must wait until the cap fully extends and the gills become colored purple-black with spores.

After removing the carpophore from the cake, cut the stem away from the mature cap as closely to the gills as possible. Place the cap right-side up on an sterilized piece of glass or paper, and cover with a cup to hold in humidity. Allow to sit for 2 days before removing the cup and the mushroom cap from the spore print. During this time, nearly all the spores should have dropped from the gills and a nice print of spores should be left behind. Store spore prints in sterile, closed containers for later use in spore solution. The cap used to achieve the spore print may then be dried for preservation, as with all other harvested carpophores.

Always dry mushrooms at a low temperature, or use desiccant to dehydrate them. Fully dried specimens are hard to the touch, with no spongy feel. Store dried specimens in a cool, dark location in air and moisture free containers.

Preparation

2 to 5 grams dried or 50 grams fresh per person are ingested. Onset of the experience is 30 to 45 minutes. Effects include open and closed eye visions, euphoria, restlessness, sleeplessness, and relaxation.

Diet Restrictions

Consult your physician before you consume this preparation if you are or may become pregnant, are nursing, or if you suffer from any chronic medical condition or are currently prescribed any medications. A minimum of a 6 hour fast should be observed prior to ingesting this preparation.

Psychotria Viridis "Chacruna"

Description

Perennial tropical bush which can reach heights exceeding 5 feet. Leaves are a glossy dark green, oval with a pointed tip, and grow to about 8 inches long and 3 to 4 inches wide. Flowers appear on long stalks and are whitish to pale green; these are succeeded by red berries that darken to black when mature. Several small brown seeds are found within the berries.

Native Habitat

Native to Cuba and southern Central America through western and central South America in the rain forests.

Preferred Growth Conditions

Prefers fertile, free-draining, acidic sandy loam in part sun. This plant is very drought tender; soil must remain moist at all times. Frost tender. If exposed to temperatures below 45 degrees F, Psychotria Viridis will die back to its roots but should recover in the spring.

Propagation

Propagates by seed and cutting. Seed should be soaked in water for 12 hours, then sown in seed trays and just covered with moist soil. Incubate trays at 70 degrees to 80 degrees F at 85% humidity or greater, in bright light. Seeds will germinate in 3 to 4 months. Seedlings may be transplanted when they reach 3 inches tall.

Cuttings are taken by removing a leaf and burying half of it in moist soil. Keep the cutting in bright light, but not direct sunlight, incubated at 75 degrees to 80 degrees F in 85% humidity or greater. Cuttings will root in 3 or 4 weeks. When new growth appears, slowly acclimate the cutting to a lower humidity. Transplant when well established.

Cultivation

Psychotria Viridis grows well in 3 to 10 gallon pots. Water frequently, but do not keep the soil soggy or allow it to dry out. Fertilize every two weeks with a balanced blend (7-7-7.) Maintain in part shade to part sun. Protect from cooler temperatures. Repot established plants every spring.

Harvest

Leaves are removed in the early morning at the peak of maturity, then dried for preservation. Take care not to defoliate the plant when harvesting leaves, and allow adequate time for re-growth between harvests. Store leaves in a dark, cool location in air and moisture free containers.

Preparation

30 grams dried leaf per person are added to twice their volume in acidified water and boiled at a low temperature for 8 hours. Liquid is then strained off and consumed. This plant preparation must be combined with B. Caapi or P. Harmala. Experience onsets 30 to 45 minutes after ingestion and lasts 4 to 6 hours. Effects typically include restlessness, closed and open eyed visions, euphoria, elated mood, and drowsiness.

Diet Restrictions

Consult your physician before you consume this plant preparation if you are or may become pregnant, are nursing, or if you suffer from any chronic medical condition or are currently prescribed any medications. This preparation must be consumed with B. Caapi or P. Harmala preparations to be effective. Read and follow the diet restriction guidelines for those plants before you consume this preparation.

Salvia Divinorum "Diviner's Sage"

Description

Perennial vine-like herb with a weak, squared stem. Can reach 6 to 10 feet in height if properly supported. Leaves are dark green with jagged edges and grow 4 to 6 inches long, and 1 to 3 inches wide. Flowers are purple and appear in spikes, but are very rarely seen. Seeds are smallish and black.

Native Habitat

Found as a cultigen in Mexico. Wild populates are extremely scarce to non-existent.

Preferred Growth Conditions

Prefers fertile, well-aerated, free-draining, acidic sandy loam in bright but filtered sunlight. Drought and frost tender. Does not grow well in low humidity or tolerate temperatures below 40 degrees F.

Propagation

Propagates by cuttings. If the plant is kept in 98% humidity for several weeks, roots will begin to appear on the leaf edges. These leaves can be removed and planted in moist soil. Maintain high humidity until it is well established and produces new growth, then slowly acclimate to lower humidity.

Alternately, a cutting may be taken by removing a branch tip with 6 sets of leaves and 4 inches of stem below the leaves. Place this cutting in water so 3.5 inches of the stalk is submerged. Maintain in a high humidity environment, and replace water every other day. Roots will appear within 2 weeks. Plant in moist soil when roots reach ¾ to 1 inch long. Keep all cuttings in bright light, but not direct sunlight. Transplant when well established.

Cultivation

Grows well in 3 to 5 gallon pots. Water frequently to keep soil moist, but do not allow the soil to remain soggy. Keep plants in indirect sunlight or in direct sunlight screened by a shading cloth. Fertilize once a week with a balanced blend (7-7-7) during the spring and summer. Salvia Divinorum will grow 4 to 6 feet a year if properly maintained. Protect from temperatures below 40 degrees F.

Harvest

Mature leaves are removed and dried, then stored in a cool, dark place in air and moisture free containers.

Preparation

½ gram dried material per person is smoked, with the material burned at a high temperature and inhaled in three successive breaths. Onset of experience is immediate and lasts 5 to 10 minutes. Effects include feeling pulled suddenly backwards and to the side, euphoria, elated mood, lethargy, closed and open eyed visions, and drowsiness.

Diet Restrictions

Consult your physician before consuming this plant preparation if you are or may become pregnant, are nursing, or if you suffer from any chronic medical condition or are currently prescribed any medications.

Tabernanthe Iboga "Iboga Root"

Description

Perennial evergreen shrub which grows 3 to 4 feet tall and 1.5 to 2.5 feet wide. Leaves are dark green on top and yellowish beneath, oval, growing to 4 inches long and 1.25 inches wide. Flowers grow in clusters of 5 to 12 and appear yellow, pink, or white spotted with pink. These are succeeded by yellow-orange fruit which appears in pairs and grows roughly to the size of an olive. Several dark brown seeds are contained in each fruit.

Native Habitat

Found in the tropical rainforests of western Africa.

Preferred Growth Conditions

Prefers fertile, free-draining, acidic loam or clay soils in part sun to full shade. Must have lots of heat and humidity to proliferate. Drought tender; soil must remain moist at all times. Frost tender; sensitive to temperatures under 40 degrees F.

Propagation

Propagates by seed. Seeds should be sown in trays and just covered with moist soil. Trays should be incubated at 90% humidity and temperatures between 80 to 85 degrees F. Sterilization of the soil is essential to prevent fungal rot of seeds. Seeds should germinate within 21 days. Seedlings may be transplanted when they reach 4 or 5 inches tall. Keep in bright light, but not direct sunlight and do not allow the soil to dry out.

Cultivation

Grows well in 25 gallon pots that have been perforated to allow for maximum drainage. Water frequently enough to keep the soil moist, but not soggy. Do not place in full sun unless a shade cloth is provided to screen the plant. Fertilize every other week with a balanced blend (7-7-7) in spring, summer, and fall. Protect from temperatures below 50 degrees F. Maintain high humidity with this plant. A greenhouse may be required to cultivate Tabernanthe Iboga in certain climates.

Harvest

Roots are harvested from 4 or 5 year old plants. The soil is dug up from around the roots, and the bush pulled free of the ground. Roots are selectively pruned, with enough left behind for the plant to survive. The bush is then replanted and not harvested from again for a full year to two years. Root clippings are thoroughly washed in water to remove all soil, then completely dried. Store in a dark, cool location in air and moisture free containers.

Preparation

4 to 6 grams root person are pulverized and ingested. Onset of experienced occurs 30 to 45 minutes after ingestion and typically lasts 25 to 30 hours. Effects include open and closed eye visions, sleeplessness, increase in body temperature and pulse, euphoria, elated mood, and lack of appetite.

Diet Restrictions

Consult your physician before consuming this plant preparation if you are or may become pregnant, are nursing, or if you suffer from any chronic medical condition or are currently prescribed any medications.

Do not combine this plant preparation with any Mono-Amine Oxidase Inhibitors. B. Caapi and P. Harmala both contain several Beta-Carboline class MAOI's, and should not be used in conjunction with this plant preparation.

Do not consume any other plant preparations than C. Sativa and N. Rustica with Tabernanthe Iboga. Observe a 10 hour fast before consuming this preparation.

Trichocereus Pachanoi "San Pedro"

Description

Perennial columnar cactus with 4 to 8 ribs which can grow to 18 feet tall in well supported stands. Spines rarely reach more than ¼ inch in length. Diameter of the column ranges from 3 to 8 inches depending on age. Flowers are white, nearly 12 inches long, very fragrant, appear on hair stalks, and only open at night. Produces no fruit, only many tiny black seeds. Trichocereus Pachanoi is not self fertile; two separate genetic strains are required to produce viable seeds.

Native Habitat

Found on the dry western slopes of the Andes in South America.

Preferred Growth Conditions

Prefers fertile, aerated, free-draining, alkaline loam or sandy loam in part shade. Very drought tolerant, but grows well with lots of moisture during the hotter seasons, sometimes adding up to 3 feet in height during one growth cycle. Frost tender; temperatures of 30 degrees F and lower will freeze the cactus and turn the growth tips black. Grows best if the soil remains dry from the late fall to early spring.

Propagation

Propagates by seed or cutting. Seeds are sown in trays containing moist sandy loam. Simply scatter seeds across the surface and do not cover with soil. Keep the tray in a 70 to 80 degree environment, in bright light but not direct sunlight, with the soil remaining moist at all times. Seeds germinate within 21 days in the proper conditions. Transplant when seedlings reach 3 to 4 inches tall; this height is usually achieved in the second year of growth.

Cuttings are taken by removing a 4 inch or longer section of cactus, slicing just below the spine pads with a sharp, sterilized knife. Allow the wound a few days to completely callous over, then place wound-side down on dry soil. Keep cutting out of direct sunlight and do not water until roots have formed. Cuttings will root within 1 to 3 months depending upon conditions. After the cutting has fully rooted, it may be watered and allowed more sunlight.

Cultivation

Grows well in wide, well-draining 5 to 25 gallon pots or in the ground in frost-free climates. Water only enough to keep the soil barely moistened. Fertilize once a month with a balanced blend (7-7-7) or brands advertised specifically for cacti in the spring and summer. Allow the soil to dry out completely in the fall and winter, with only occasional misting to provide hydration. Full sun may burn this cactus. This is evidenced by the cactus turning from green to a purple or red color. If this occurs, allow the cactus to have more shade. Protect from temperatures of 35 degrees F and lower. Does well when maintained as a house plant during the winter in colder climates.

Harvest

Sections are removed with a sharp knife in the same fashion as a cutting. This section is left to sit in indirect sunlight for 2 months before use.

Preparation

3 pounds per person, approximately a 1 foot long, 4 inch diameter section, is sliced into thin discs, just covered with water, and boiled at a low temperature for 4 hours. The water is then filtered off and consumed. Alternately, the ribs of the cactus

may be removed from the core and processed with a vegetable juicer, with the juices consumed.

Diet Restrictions

Consult your physician before using this plant preparation if you are or may become pregnant, are nursing, or if you suffer from any chronic medical condition or are currently prescribed medication.

Do not combine this plant preparation with any Mono-Amine Oxidase Inhibitors. B. Caapi and P. Harmala preparations both contain several Beta-Carboline class MAOI's, and should not be used in conjunction with this plant preparation.

Do not use in combination with Lophophora Williamsii preparation. Observe a minimum of a 6 hour fast before consuming this plant preparation.

Proper Use of the Sacred Teacher Plants

The Sacred Teacher Plants should only be used as part of a ritual. Do not consume these casually, as this will upset their Spirits. Take care not to perform any ritual with these plants unless you have established the proper mindset and setting, and only as part of your own Spiritual advancement or to assist another with the same. If you respect these plants, they will respect you. Tend your garden well, and these Sacred Teacher Plants will cultivate you as well as you have them.

Section 4:

Magic Manual

Introduction

This manual is written simply as a guide. It is not the final answer to Magical techniques or feats which may be performed by Magic. Some or all of these techniques may or may not work for you, and some you will find success with only when you are in the most dire of necessity. These are merely suggested methods for employing the ends described; feel free to alter the method or end as you see fit.

In the working of Magic and the Path of the Shaman, it is important that you walk your own Path. Advice given to you by others can only be presented from their perspective, and that same advice is limited by their ability to communicate with you and your ability to understand them. Nothing conferred is understood exactly in the same manner as the one who presents it wishes it to be understood. You must walk your own Path, see it for yourself rather than take as absolute anything ever taught to you, and overcome your own obstacles in your own way. This approach to life is the Way of the Shaman itself; Magic Rituals and the rest are little more than trappings. With that stated, welcome to the practice of Magic, and the best of luck on your journey.

Conjuring Images

With dedicated practice, it is possible to form the Plane of Imagination so strongly that the perceptions of others are drawn to it, and regard it as if it were Material. The first step to working in this branch of Magic is to quell the Emotions and the random Images that flow through your mind. Only with steadfast thought and a peaceful Emotional current can you consciously form and hold forms of Imagination. This quietude of Soul is best garnered through the daily practices of Following the Breath and Five Gates Breathing.

This first exercise will introduce you to Imagery techniques and prepare you for more detailed workings in Conjuring by directing you in the process of forming a globe within the palm of your hand. It is helpful to practice this with as minimal disturbances as possible; however, shutting out the world is impossible and learning to work with disturbances is much more practical. Learning to work with distractions and actually bend those distractions to aid you in your work of Magic will help you gain a high degree of proficiency in all the areas of Magic.

Exercise 1: Forming a Globe

1. Begin by seating yourself comfortably in an area set aside for Magic practice. If it aids your relaxation, burn candles and incense. These are not necessary items for this practice, however.

2. Relax your mind and body. Allow your breathing to settle into a calm rhythm. Set aside your daily troubles for the time being, and relax your body completely.

3. Hold your hands in your lap as if you were holding a ball about the size of a grapefruit. If you feel it will help, close your eyes at this point.

4. Form the ball in your hands. Feel its weight, a few pounds, and its smooth, cool surface. Lift it a bit to feel how heavy it is, then roll it between your palms. Continue rolling it from one palm to the other until you've developed a good feel for it.

5. Gaze at the ball. It is clear, like crystal, with a slightly bluish tint to it. Its surface is bright, reflective, and its center contains imperfections. Roll the ball around in your palms slowly, gazing into it until you can see all its imperfections, and you know its shape, weight, and visual appearance.

6. Unless you are capable of holding its form perfectly, it will change with your thoughts. Do not let this disturb you, but practice holding it in the same form for extended periods of time. When you grow tired from practice, simply Will the ball away.

This exercise, as most others do, will expend the Ether your body typically converts to Life Fire. Do not over-practice. Also remember that this ball you have created is not real. It is an illusion; when you are able to influence others into seeing it, you are creating a hallucination for them. If you feel you must test your ability upon others(which is ill-advised, especially for beginners,) do not inform them that you are going to attempt to create something for them to see with your Will. Their Will can do little more at that point than conflict with yours. Be subtle when you use this technique, no matter what the circumstances may be.

Exercise 2: Conjuring a Butterfly

This exercise is a more advanced practice than forming a globe and should only be attempted when success has been found with the globe. This exercise will also expend a greater amount of Ether than the previous exercise, so make certain that you are not in need of rest or recharging when you practice.

1. Begin by seating yourself comfortably in your place of Magical workings. Do those things which aid in your comfort and ability to draw power.
2. Settle your mind and body, and allow the worries of the normal day to drain away from you. Allow your breath to reach an easy pace, and cup your hands gently in your lap.

3. In your hands, feel a butterfly land. Feel the light tickle of its feet, and the tiny breath of air as it slowly flutters its wings.

4. Look at the butterfly. It faces away from you, with its wings slowly spreading and drawing back together. Note the color patterns of its wings; blue, orange, red, and green. Also examine its body in detail; its antenna, legs, and torso.

5. Continue gazing at the butterfly until you can see it with the utmost precision of detail.

6. Have the butterfly walk around your palms, then over to the back of your hand. Work with this aspect until you are able to sense and control each of its footsteps and every flutter of its wings.

7. When you have completed your practice for the evening, have it walk up your forefinger and then fly away, disappearing midair.

If the object you are Conjuring disappears on you during practice, don't fret. These exercises will help you train your ability to control the Plane of Imagination; chances are that before now, you never consciously attempted to form anything to this extent. Do not take a mistake as a failure; it is a chance to learn and a necessary experience if you are to gain mastery over this branch of Magic.

Once you feel you have mastered the conjuration of these two simple forms of globe and butterfly, experiment with ideas of your own. It is important for your development that you expand upon your creative insights and work to refine your technique and perspective in all branches of Magic. Do not do work to impress others; only do that which feels proper and impress yourself by working in this manner.

As a side note, if you train with seriousness and treat the training as work, you will not be as relaxed and flexible as you can be. Train and practice in ways that are play to you; be dedicated, but not rigidly serious. The only wrong way to practice and exercise is by not doing it all, so have fun with it and modify your exercises into a form that enables you to play with it.

Exercise 3: The Cloak of Shadows

This exercise will introduce you to a technique that allows you to cloak yourself in a shadow of perceptions. As with the rest of Conjuration of Imagination, it does not literally create shade over you. Instead, this technique helps others to overlook you by blending you into the rest of the insignificant details of the background. In darkened areas, this technique can render you nearly invisible to anyone, and at times even so to those who are actively searching for you.

1. Begin by forming a Magic Circle. Fast-cast Circles are also effective for this technique.
2. Clear your mind. Any strong thoughts or bodily tension can give you away while cloaking yourself.
3. Form an Image of a wavering fabric in front of you. This fabric is flexible and will stretch to cover your entire form; it feels

slick and is barely translucent. It appears black, but it disappears in spots and patches that roll across the fabric. It constantly changes, and there are sometimes dim colors seen that change black.

4. Wrap yourself within the fabric. This is the Cloak of Shadows. Part your Circle and carry on your task or hiding.

When using the Cloak of Shadows, it is highly important that your thoughts are still. Practice creating this frequently if you intend to use it with skill; it is possible to hide entire groups of people, vehicles, and houses if you have prepared yourself. Keep your Will directed at the Cloak as long as you use it, and it will not fail as long as you do not waver.

Exercise 4: Changing the Façade

This exercise is three-part and will help you gradually work your way through changing your appearance by Conjuration. This can help people to not recognize you, or to recognize you as someone else as the situation calls for. Keep in mind that this technique will not actually change the way you look, but only mask what is truly present. It is also possible to modify this technique for use with objects if you feel the need to do so and practice with it. The degree of difficulty for exercising this technique in front of others is based upon the keenness of their perception, how much scrutiny yourself or the object at hand is under, and your ability to hold the form for them to perceive.

Exercise 4 Part A: Masking the Eyes

It is possible to change your eye color to make them appear impressive or unimpressive, or just downright different from your normal color. With the implication of contact lenses today, many will find this technique to be useless; however, practice with this technique does allow for rapid changing of different practiced forms. This technique is a beginning point for the rest of this exercise, and should not be overlooked.

1. Begin by forming your Magic Circle. Have a small mirror with you when you do.
2. Clear your mind and relax your body. Seat yourself in the Circle for practice.
3. Form an image of brilliant amber eyes, piercing, that seem to generate a cold heat. Cover your eyes with this form, until you feel that your eyes have become this.
4. Pick up the mirror and gaze at your eyes while holding the form over them. Continue practicing with this technique until you can clearly see the form you have placed over your eyes.
5. When you have finished practice, part your Circle and eat.

Continue practicing this exercise until you can summon up the amber eyes at Will. If you can think of another type of form you would like to use, work with it as well. When you create forms, try for those which will be useful rather than impressive. If you attempt to generate a form for its impressive effect with little other in mind than impressing others, you will fall short of your goal. Also remember that when you stop holding the form solid, it disappears. For others to view it, you must be able to hold it for vast lengths of time with no quivering of your attention.

Exercise 4 Part B: Masking the Facial Structure

This part of the exercise will allow you to train yourself in transforming the appearance of facial features such as the nose, chin, cheekbones, eyebrows, and even skin tone. The depth to which you form these changes is only limited by your creativity and your ability to hold that form.

1. Form a Magic Circle. Make certain that you have a small mirror with you.
2. Seat yourself comfortably in the Circle. Calm your thoughts and relax your body.
3. Envision your face as it is; if you cannot recall your own face, use the mirror to assist you.
4. Begin with your chin. Using your Will, broaden it until it appears to be nearly square, and pull it outwards a bit from your face.

5. After shaping your chin to your satisfaction, follow the jaw line on your face and have it grow until it is powerful and prominent. Your chin and jaw should look much larger than normal now, and almost ogrish. Practice holding the form while opening and closing your mouth and gazing at your new countenance in the mirror.

6. When you are successful with the jaw and chin, turn to your cheekbones. Will them to appear sunken, with little nubs for mounds.

7. Next, work with your forehead. Draw the base at the eyebrows outwards, broadening it, and have it slope upwards to the hairline. Examine yourself in the mirror and practice holding this form.

8. Part your Circle and eat to complete this exercise.

The form detailed in this exercise will help you to change the appearance of your face into the likeness of what some would call a "caveman." There is little likelihood that this specific façade will be useful to you in day to day affairs, but using it will confuse others when you wish for your identity to be remembered less accurately. You should think up your own special appearance if you wish to use this technique frequently, and practice it accordingly.

It is possible to use a smaller version of the "Cloak of Shadows" to cover your face so that your features remain unnoticed. Its swirling darkness tends to distract attention away from your features, making them seem inconsequential. You may wish to practice with this technique on your own; ingenuity and adaptation will help you find the best way to practice this.

Exercise 4 Part C: Masking the Body Structure

The purpose of this exercise is to change the overall appearance of the body. This technique can be utilized for intimidation, to reduce threat by appearance, or just to mask your true self. As with all other exercises, the form you practice the most will be the easiest for you to utilize.

1. Form a Magic Circle. Do not sit; this exercise is best practiced while standing.
2. Relax yourself completely. Your mind and body must reach a state of quiet, and your breath should settle into a deepened, slow pace of its own.
3. Feel yourself shrink to half of your normal size. You do not feel more frail or as though you have lost strength. Your size in relation to your surroundings is all that should change.
4. With your mind remaining clear and your Will focused upon your size reduction, examine yourself. Look about you at the objects around you. With

success, you will notice that your relevant size appears smaller than it did before, whereas the objects around you appear much larger.

5. Practice this exercise until you begin to feel tired. If your focus of Will is lost and you lose the illusion at any point, begin again until you feel you are either too exhausted or too frustrated to continue. Do not force the illusion; you will be able to work it with ease given a sufficient quantity of effort.

For all to witness the appearance you have constructed for yourself, you must practice consistently. With sufficient effort, you will master this technique and be able to use it with skillful ease. Be creative when you "sketch out" a form you would like to mask yourself with, and if you have the opportunity, fuel it with strong Emotion. This will help your forms to hold more substance, even under intense scrutiny. No matter what your degree of success, however, there will always be at least one individual who will see you as you are and not as your covering.

Spectres, Doppelgangers, and Lycanthropy

Spirits can reveal themselves in the form of a Spectre. This form is assumed by the Spirit Conjuring a form for itself upon the Plane of Imagination with enough force for even untrained individuals to view. Spectres are generally perceived as fleeting wisps of shadows which gather and disperse quickly and repeatedly, or only appear on the edge of sight. Not all Spirits which use these forms are unbound to the Material Plane; at times, individuals gather these forms without awareness when traveling "out of body." This form can be useful for repelling intruders, and can be set up as a defense mechanism during sleep.

Exercise 5: Forming the Spectre

1. Cast your Magic Circle. Speak aloud your intentions to the Spirits; welcome them to aid you in your cause.

2. Remain standing within your Circle, and regulate your breath and thoughts until you reach a state of deep quietude.

3. Visualize a starting point at the perimeter of the area you wish to defend. Begin to walk it, slowly, observing with care each step you make and the area you walk through. As you walk, leave a line of burning blue Ether at the perimeter. Continue this until you have walked the entire perimeter and you are back where you began.

4. Expand your perception until you can see from where you physically are to the Etheric boundary you have formed. At this point, Will a dark shadow to flit around the boundary, following the line. Watch the Spectre follow the line until you are satisfied you have applied enough force (but don't try to force it) for it to sustain itself in the deep of your psyche.

5. Thank the Spirits for their assistance in this matter, offering them whatever feels correct to you for their aid.

6. Part your Circle and eat, knowing that your boundary is erected and strong.

This boundary is most effect when renewed nightly. It is possible to weave a strong Emotion into it, such as Fear, to add to the effect any who reach the Etheric line will experience. Not all will see the Spectre you have generated, but it will guard the line by "pushing" any who approach it unwelcome away.

The Doppelganger is very similar to the Spectre in usage by Spirits and individuals on an O.B.E. (out-of-body-experience,) but it is a much more detailed and stronger formation of the Plane of Imagination. Spirits who use this form are generally possessed of a greater deal of energy than those who use the wisps. One of the advantages of the Doppelganger over the Spectre is its potency of perception; even highly critical individuals can view it quite clearly when they come into contact with one.

Exercise 6: Forming the Doppelganger

1. Begin by casting your Magic Circle. Seat yourself in the middle.
2. Allow your breath and thoughts to settle until you are completely relaxed.
3. Place your perception a bit in front of you, at your standing level. Hold it firmly there until you can do it with ease.
4. With your perception away from your Material Manifestation, look down at your hands. Take your time viewing each one until you can see them in complete detail.

5. Look down at the rest of your body, beginning with your arms and shoulders, then dropping your gaze until it reaches your feet. You will notice that you appear as you Will yourself to at this point.

6. Feel your hair, the back of your head, and your face to familiarize yourself with them.

7. Once you have familiarized yourself with the form of your Doppelganger, walk around. If you wish to react to an object as solid in this state it will be so, but you may also pass through solid objects. Practice walking around and looking at things until you are able to do this with ease.

8. It is possible to travel in this form by flinging your perception to an area. This is accomplished by application of Will. Move to a distant location now.

9. Once again, practice walking around and looking at items in detail until you can do it easily and comfortably.

10. Return your perception to your body while maintaining perceptions from the point of your Doppelganger. Practice maintaining both until you are comfortable doing so.

11. Once you are capable of maintaining both, practice moving one without the other, then try moving both your body and the Doppelganger in different ways until you are proficient in so doing.

12. Part your Circle and eat to end this exercise.

If at any time during this practice you feel like you have lost your Doppelganger or perception, begin again by forming it just in front of you and familiarizing yourself with its appearance. Form an appearance which is strong first before you attempt to move around and observe items. Before attempting to travel distances, make certain that you can easily walk around and observe. These are important steps if you wish to use this technique with proficiency. It is possible for highly advanced practitioners to form multiple Doppelgangers and send them out to different locations simultaneously, or to surround yourself with Doppelgangers in the event of danger. However, do not even attempt this if you are not able to walk around with one and observe items far away while still performing mundane tasks with your body.

Lycanthropy is a technique very similar in practice to both Masking the Body and forming a Doppelganger. This Magic skill allows you to assume the form of a man beast, typically of a wolf, bear, or deer and requires a headdress and cloak of the same. Ayahuasca and San Pedro teas are highly effective in amplifying the strength of the illusion cast with this exercise, but should only be utilized after several successful practices.

Exercise 7: Conjuring the Form of the Lycanthrope

1. Begin by assembling your attire. Headdress, cloak or jacket, and belt of the animal hide along with black face and body paint of the form you wish to assume are necessities.

2. Form your Magic Circle. If you will be using Sacred Plants with this exercise, consume them after forming your Circle.

3. While standing, relax your breath, body, and thought process.

4. Feel the hide meld with your body, and the perception of your normal form change with it. Your head and face take on characteristics more closely to the animal you have chosen, and your arms and torso take on a combination of the two. Your legs remain very closely in resemblance to normal, except becoming more furry.

5. Examine yourself, and see yourself as you wish to appear. Keep your thoughts clear, and your Will focused upon the Lycanthropic form.

6. Leave your Circle and accomplish the task you have set out for yourself. When it is completed, return to the Circle, thank the Spirit of the animal for its help and offering whatever gifts you deem necessary to it.

7. Relinquish the form and return to your normal one, disrobe. Part your Circle and eat.

The form of any animal in combination with your typical appearance may be assumed by use of this technique as long as you have practiced sufficiently with that animal form and you have the proper materials. For highly advanced practitioners, it is possible to Conjure up this appearance for yourself without the use of any animal hide. When utilizing this skill, it is possible that you may feel compelled to act upon the normal instincts of the animal you have chosen; if this occurs outside of your Circle, return to it and relinquish the form immediately.

This exercise on Lycanthropy concludes the section on Conjuration of the Imagination. If you wish to develop strong skills in this area of Magical practice, you must exercise on a regular basis. These seven exercises offered are not all that is possible with this branch of Magic; with creativity and effort, you will discover many more techniques on your own.

Elemental Magic

This is perhaps the most difficult section of Magic in general to develop any degree of skill over as it takes both a significant quantity of practice and almost if not total dissolution of the illusion of "within and without." Despite this, the following exercises in this section can be very useful for helping you gain a greater understanding on the way energy constructs the Seventh Plane world around. Do not despair if you do not find immediate success; competent practice will allow this area to eventually unfold for your usage when you are prepared.

The Elemental State

The next exercise involves working with the Plane of Imagination in order to orient you with the feeling of and the ability to change the Elemental State of an item. These elemental states are referred to as Air, Earth, Fire, and Water. Each can be converted from one to the other, if you work through the progression of the bonds of radiating and gravitating. These Elemental States refer to the balance of gravitating and radiating in an Elemental Manifestation and not to the specific Elemental Manifestation itself.

Earth is the most gravitating of these four, and possesses little to no sense of radiating. When the radiating is increased in Earth, it becomes Water, which possesses enough gravitation to hold itself together. Air, one radiating step up from Water, can only hold itself together loosely. When the gravitating is almost if not completely eliminated, Fire is found, which disperses quickly unless converted to another form.

Exercise 1: Changing the Elemental State

1. Begin by forming your Magic Circle. Seat yourself in its center, relax your body, breath, and thoughts, and close your eyes.

2. Shift your perception to the 5th Plane. Begin orienting yourself by visualizing your body and your Magic Circle.

3. Once you are properly oriented, looked down at your hands and Will a ball of smooth granite into your palms. Examine it and familiarize yourself with its qualities before progressing.

4. Feel within the ball of granite for the bonds that hold it together. They feel like a strong force, almost magnetic, and are accompanied by a deep toned "electric" buzzing sound. Observe the force and the sound, and when you are able, explore for yourself what its quality of light is.

5. When you are able to grasp the bonds, expand them. The tone will raise in pitch and frequency, and the force will begin to feel more rubbery. The light of the bonds will also increase. When you are successful, the granite ball will seem to feel like mud at first, and then turn to a liquid. Hold it in the spherical shape with your Will, and it will remain as such.

6. Familiarize yourself with the bonds in the Water state. Once you are familiar, raise it again into the Air State. You will find that in this state, the granite ball must be held into shape and place with your Will.

7. Examine the bonds in the Air Elemental State, and when you are prepared, expand them once again into Fire. The granite ball will not increase in temperature or actually burn, but it will be more difficult to contain it with your Will. Do not allow it to escape the shape you are compelling it to maintain.

8. With success in the Fire Elemental State, work your way back down to Air, then Water, then Earth. Return the granite ball to the place from whence it came.

9. Open your eyes and return your perception to the Seventh Plane. Part your Circle, and eat to conclude this exercise.

Practice this exercise nightly for as long as it takes for you to feel you have mastered it. The feeling you get from practicing this on the 5th Plane carries over to the 7th Plane. The bonds are the same and react the same way on both Planes. The main difficulty with working this class of Magic on the 7th Plane is the fact that you are fighting against the Will of many who would that Magic was not, although it is. Practice until your results are consistently successful and you will be able to apply it to the Material Plane.

Manipulating Energies of the Material Plane

This next section will be composed of exercises towards training you to manipulate 7th Plane energies. These energies include but are not limited to kinetic, light, and heat. All 7th Plane energies are an expression of RF (Radio Frequency). To learn more about the different frequencies of radio, please consult scientific documentation.

Exercise 2: Influencing the Candle Flame

1. Prepare a place to sit comfortably. This space should include a candle of any color, and a structure upon which the candle will rest at approximately chest height. The candle must be placed far enough away so that your breath will not disturb it. Likewise, the area should be relatively free of breeze so the flame does not dance about.

2. Relax your body, breath, and thoughts. A Magic Circle is unnecessary for this exercise.

3. Observe the flame. Reach out with your perception until you can feel the flame as it feels itself. To successfully move the flame, you must become one with it.

4. When you feel you are able, rotate the flame clockwise. If it feels heavy, do not try to force it; gently push it and it will begin to turn in the direction you Will.

5. With success in rotating the flame clockwise, reverse the direction. Practice this until you are able to do it with ease.

6. Now stretch the flame upwards. Elongate it as much as you are able, and then press it downwards. Do this slowly, taking as much time as you need. It is possible, if you are too hasty, to fling the fire into your ceiling or down into the floor. Relax and work patiently with the flame.

7. If you wish, you may continue this exercise by tipping the flame towards the compass points. When you perform this, work in a circular direction rather than going to opposites.

8. Conclude this exercise by blowing out the candle, taking a few deep, penetrating breaths, and stretching lightly.

This exercise should be performed nightly until you are able to manipulate the flame with ease. Upon success, if you wish to maintain your skills, practice at least twice weekly if only for a few moments. Those who develop Mastery over this skill will find it possible to form a raging inferno almost instantly from a spark, with nearly any fuel for the fire.

Exercise 3: Influencing the Pendulum

1. Obtain a free-hanging pendulum with a stand. Prepare a place for you to sit with this apparatus where it will not be disturbed by wind or intense vibrations.

2. Seat yourself in front of the pendulum and relax yourself. Take a few deep breaths and clear your thoughts. When you are clear, reach into the pendulum with your perception and feel it as it is.

3. You will find a center of force within the pendulum. This force is moving, but only slightly, in a clockwise elliptical pattern. Experience the force until you are one with it.

4. When you understand the nature of the force within the pendulum, you have become it and you will be able to increase it. Gently feed energy into the pendulum until it is visibly moving.

5. Maintain the motion of the pendulum until there is no difficulty for you to do so.

6. Allow the pendulum to stop visibly moving. Now, change the force within so the pendulum begins to swing in the opposite direction. This part of the exercise can be quite challenging.

7. Maintain this direction of swing until it is no longer difficult for you to do so.

8. Allow the pendulum to come to its rest. Now swing it back and forth, towards yourself and away. When you are able to do this with ease, swing it from side to side.

9. End this exercise by taking a few deep, penetrating breaths, and stretching lightly.

Similar versions of this exercise can be performed with a billiards ball on a table or floor. Remember to place whatever you are working with away from drastic influence by any forces outside of your own Will. Practice this exercise nightly until you are able to perform it with ease. It may take a few months before you see any definite progress, but don't despair; if you practice with determination, you will be well rewarded.

Exercise 4: Binding the Light

1. Obtain a small mirror. Prepare a place for you to sit in which you can look into the mirror without seeing your own reflection.

2. Relax your body, breath, and thoughts. Peer into the mirror. Do not look deeply into the mirror; what you seek is the light surface, which is actually just a bit above the glass.

3. Once you find this layer, shift your perception into it until you become one with it. Feel the flow of the light towards and away from the mirror. Understand its nature by experiencing it.

4. You will notice nearly all of the light that reaches this layer bounces away from it geometrically. This reflection gives the mirror its silvery quality. Slow down the light flowing away from the mirror.

5. As you slow down the reflection, you will notice the mirror begins to dim significantly. Continue until the mirror has become a flat, non reflective blackness. The light continues to strike the mirror surface, but it goes no further. Hold this blackness until you are able to do this with ease.

6. Now, slowly return the reflection to the mirror. Practice darkening the mirror once again. Continue this process until there is no difficulty for you.

This exercise can be taken a step further by darkening objects, or by taking a powerful beam of light from a flood lamp or flashlight and bending its beam in different directions as you Will. Practice this exercise nightly until you are able to easily perform it if you wish to master it, and to maintain your skill, practice at least once or twice a week.

This concludes the section on Elemental Magics. These are not the only possible Magical feats that may be performed under this section of Magic, but they are the most practical. Due to the nature of the Shroud, it has become increasingly difficult in this day and age to actually summon items, or hurl fire and lightning from your fingertips. These feats are not impossible, but are quite impractical for practice and use in your daily life.

Feel free to improvise and work with your ideas in this and all other sections. Magic is as you Will it to be.

Emotional Empathic Magic

This section will deal with Magic based upon sensing and suggesting Emotional States in other individuals. To some degree, will all use these skills in our day to day affairs with all other beings, though you may or may not be aware of this. For those who are aware of this and practice, much can be done to influence and understand others.

Sensing the Emotional State of another is impossible if you are too concerned with yourself. Your thoughts and Emotions must be calmed, and not suppressed for you to feel the flow of Emotions which surges from all other beings. For this reason, it is highly recommended that those of you who wish to pursue mastery of this skill practice Following the Breath diligently. There is little to be offered in the way of practicing Empathy other than this: understand yourself first, and listen to others. There is no other way to be truly Empathic.

The Suggestive Presence

Emotional Energy constantly streams outwards from all things. Your Emotional Temper is the way these Emotions affect you, and the way you respond in manipulating these Energies as they flow away from you. When you are able to sense and command the Emotions you radiate, you are able to influence the way others respond to you. This area of Emotional Empathic Magic is termed "The Suggestive Presence."

Exercise 1: The Presence of Lust

This exercise will enable you to pour out Emotions that stimulate lust, or the desire for sex, in other individuals. Each individual you stimulate with this Energy will react in a different way; if the feelings you stir within them force them to confront sexual issues they are attempting to suppress, you could be facing an extremely angry or nervous individual. If they are content with these feelings and welcome them, they could fling themselves upon you or lose control of themselves in the desire to rut. Practice all of these exercises with caution.

1. Prepare yourself by bathing and dressing appropriately. Make certain that you do not smell strongly and are generally kempt in appearance. Take time to meditate before going out to practice, and be certain that no troubling issues confront you during your practice. It is also wise for a beginner to not practice this while in communion with the Sacred Plants, though for an adept or master, those Spirits can enhance the experience.

2. Go out into a place where you can socialize with others, where it would not be unduly strange for you to introduce yourself to strangers or imposing upon those with whom you are already acquainted. When you meet the person you wish to suggest, maintain good eye contact, only tracing the outline of their body in a way that will compliment them. Speak calmly and as little as possible. Encouraging them to speak will

place them in a more receptive state to harmonize with the Energies you will bestow upon them.

3. You must feel no Emotion while doing this; you must simply become the embodiment of the feeling of lust. The feeling you will find brings you the most success is the same as the one generated by an orgasm in its peak. You will not be in orgasm, or feeling the pleasure; you must become it and pour it into their center. The Emotional Energy Center you wish to stream this energy into is their Heart Center.

4. Once you find they are readily absorbing the Emotion you pour into them, light caresses (when the individual welcomes it) will enhance the quantity of Energy you stream into them. Massage is also an effective way to dramatically increase the amount of energy you are able to pour into them.

5. End this exercise by thanking them for the time they have spent upon you, and sharing with them how pleasant of an experience you thought it was. At this point, it is highly important to beam a sensation of Emotional warmth, or Love, into them. This aspect of the technique allows their Temper to be motivated towards sharing Love with more people, including those they would have previously not been inclined to do so for.

An alternate way to present this Presence is by extending Auric Tendrils soaked with the Emotion you wish to invoke. As you walk by others, their natural tendency to touch your aura will imbed the sensation within them. This is a highly effective technique for increasing your sexual attractiveness to others.

Practice this technique with everyone you meet, whether or not you would wish to have sex with them, unless you see it makes them uncomfortable. This will help to develop your skills in working with others, and influencing them in what would be viewed as a positive way. Mastery of this skill is not a license to go out and seduce as many as you can; use your skills with wisdom and precocious care.

<u>Exercise 2: The Presence of Terror</u>

Like the Presence of Lust, the Presence of Terror is highly effective in suggesting certain modes of behavior with other individuals. It can be used to ward away trouble, such as a physical conflict with any type of animal, or simply if you wish to be undisturbed. You will find that if you constantly radiate this Presence, others will find it highly difficult and ultimately disturbing to be around you or communicate with you for any period of time.

1. Prepare yourself by bathing, dressing appropriately, and making certain that you do not smell strongly. Take a bit of time to meditate and relax your thoughts before you go out.
2. When you meet a person you wish to intimidate or terrify, your eyes must be drawn strongly open. The Energies with this technique seem to

stream from the eyes, and wrap about the throat of the other, strangling them.

3. Speak as little as possible. From your eyes, intense bursts of Emotional pain and coldness must pour into the other. Continue streaming this into them until they have cowed or fled.

It is sometimes helpful to visualize the person you are intimidating with a mauled visage, screaming, or crying. Take care when you use this technique with others; some will take it as an invitation to violence, while others can be psychically damaged by it. Only utilize this skill out of absolute necessity.

Many different Emotions and feelings can be conveyed using variances of this technique. Take the time to work with feelings you wish to generate in others, and observe both yourself and others to see how they flow away from you and into them. Placing more impetus upon the natural route of these energies will enable you to enhance their flow.

Emotional Wyrms

When a person or item is thought of with strong intention, many times a Wyrm, or wave of Emotional Energy, flows outwards with the thought and strikes the object. With practice and observation, these Wyrms can be directed with Will. Care must be taken when utilizing this approach, however; the Wyrm will not always rest upon the target, and can strike one whom you were not intending. For this reason, clarity in vision of the one whom you wish to receive the Wyrm must be achieved with the utmost precision.

Wyrms can be helpful or hurtful. It is discouraged that you place hurtful Wyrms within people, as these most often can only be removed by intensive psychical work within the individual. The next two exercises will deal with forming Wyrms, and removing those which have been implanted in others.

Exercise 3: Forming the Wyrm

1. Begin by forming a Magic Circle.
2. Seat yourself in the center of the Circle, relax your body, breath and thoughts.
3. Why do you wish to form this Wyrm? You must evaluate this question thoroughly before proceeding.
4. With this answer in mind, visualize the person at whom you are directing the Wyrm. Shift your perception into them, until you become one with them.
5. Cup your palms. Into them, allow the Emotion you wish to form the Wyrm with to flow. As the Emotion flows into your palms, the Wyrm will form. If it is a beneficial Wyrm, it will appear as an electric blue. If it is a maleficent Wyrm, it will appear electric red.
6. After the Wyrm has been formed, direct it to fly to the person within whom you are implanting it. Allow it to sink into the part of the person's body where its presence will be most conducive to the end you have in mind. Every

time you see the person from this point on, view the Wyrm. This will help you to reinforce its presence.

7. Conclude this technique by first clearing your mind of it, then part your Circle and eat.

Forming and implanting Wyrms can be quite helpful in assisting a chronically ill person, be it mental or physical, recover from their illness. There are many different situations in which a Wyrm can be used, more for healing than for injuring. Use this technique with cautious wisdom.

Exercise 4: Removing a Wyrm

Unfortunately, many Wyrms are released by those dwelling upon vengeful and hurtful thoughts. The most unfortunate part of this is that many of these Wyrms that were intended to hurt a certain individual do not ever reach that individual. Small children are most often the victims of these illness-causing Emotional waves. Thankfully, there are ways for a Shaman to remove these Wyrms from an infected person, as well as to help the person work through any Auric damages that may have been incurred upon exposure to it.

1. Begin by forming a Magic Circle around the person to be healed and yourself. Ask the person to relax and guide them through a bit of deep

breathing, and take a moment to clear your own thoughts and relax your body.

2. From the palms, generate an electric-arc type flow of Ether into the body of the injured party. This flow should feel slightly cool and soothing, and will entice the Wyrm to exit the body of the person in whom it is lodged. When enough Ether has been applied, the Wyrm will flow into you.

3. After the Wyrm has flowed into you, take a few moments to change its energy. Go to a place where you can be alone until this has been accomplished. There are two ways this can be performed; either coax the Wyrm into the Earth to be transmuted, or transmute it within your own energy system from the angry red into a powdery white, and then into the electric blue Ether.

4. Once transmutation has occurred, return to the injured party, who should have remained in the Circle this whole time. Speak with them about people they may have intentionally or unintentionally wronged. Encourage them to find a solution to the situation in which their and the Emotional Temper of any others involved will have improved.

5. Part the Circle and eat, drink, or share communion by way of the Sacred Plants with the person from whence the Wyrm was removed.

Some Shamans prefer to perform this technique during rituals with the Sacred Plants. If you are familiar with this technique and have used it before, utilizing Sacred

Plants is highly encouraged. The Spirits will often lend a helping hand both to you and to the injured party when you invite them to in this way. It can also be a beneficial time for the injured party to completely heal rifts in their Aura which were caused by Emotional trauma and have yet to close.

This concludes the section on Emotional Empathic Magic. Many variations of this techniques will be found by those of you who choose to explore the creative possibilities of your own mind. Do not be limited solely to the exact techniques listed here, and take those that you do choose to incorporate into your daily life fairly and passionately.

Enchantment

Enchantment is the branch of Magic in which selected energy is stored within an Elemental Manifestation. This Emotional Energy stored within the item emanates from it profusely, and in addition to the normal type of energy transmuted by the object. The technique of Enchanting an object creates a powerful tool that continues to generate results long after the Magical process is performed.

Enchanted items are generally referred to as Charms, but it is also possible to forge enchanted symbols, which are typically referred to as Runes. Charms and Runes both have the same goal in mind- infusion with an abundance of a specific vibration to influence the environment. Some goals of this infusion are: to increase sexual desirability; to bring "good luck" both by affecting the perspective of situations and by attracting beneficial circumstances; or to ward away malevolent influences and those generating the same. It is also possible to form those conducive to better health and longevity. Regardless of whether you are utilizing a Charm or Rune, and no matter what your goal is, the process is the same. The next several exercises will introduce you to the technique of Enchantment.

Exercise 1: Prayer Beads for Peace

1. Obtain string, approximately two feet in length, and 33 beads to cover the same.

2. Form a Magic Circle. Invite all Spirits to attend and lend their powers to assist you if they Will. Offer these same Spirits gifts of thankfulness for their presence.

3. Seat yourself in the center of your Circle. Take a few moments to meditate and find a relaxation of body, breath, and mind.

4. Become the Emotional Energy or feeling you wish to evoke. In this instance, it will be Placitude. Pick three words which strongly express this feeling for you.

5. Tie a knot at one end of the string to hold the beads. As you string the beads, continue to be the feeling of Placitude and say one of the words you wish to weave into the Charm. Keep the words in order, and have each bead become the word and the feeling of the word you place upon it.

6. Continue stringing the Prayer Beads on the string until all are placed. When all are placed, knot the other end of the string to hold the beads into place.

7. With the Charm assembled, take as long as necessary until your Will has forged the Prayer Beads into the feeling of Placitude itself.

8. Stand, and thank the Spirits for their attendance. Ask of them to accept your gifts as true thankfulness for their assistance and observation.

9. Part your Circle, then eat.

This item will never lose its "charge" unless it is changed by yourself or another entity. Whenever you touch the Beads, invoke the feeling of Placitude. If you are in a stressful situation during which you are having difficulty accessing this feeling, take the time to touch each bead singularly and recite the word you have bound upon it.

The more this process is performed upon an item, the "stronger" it becomes. When you have stored enough energy within it, it will cause a ripple in the Emotional Energies of any area it lies within it, transmuting them to Placitude. Dedicate time and effort to repeat this process with the beads, and you will notice a change in the way people react to its presence.

Exercise 2: The Amulet of Benevolence

It is not always necessary to craft the item you wish to Enchant, though it can be very helpful to storing energies within it. This exercise will instruct you in Enchanting an item you have not manufactured, and that you may wear as a necklace.

1. Obtain a necklace with an amulet, pendant, or other piece of adornment which you can wear comfortably.

2. Form a Magic Circle. Invite all Spirits to attend and take part in the Magical crafting of this piece. Offer them gifts of thankfulness for their part.

3. Seat yourself in the middle of the Circle. Take a few moments to relax your body, breath and mind.

4. Become the feeling of Benevolence. This feeling should be the same type of caring that a devoted parent bestows upon their child, or that a leader bestows upon their followers.

5. Pour this feeling into the Amulet, with the item held in your hands. Do not clasp the item tightly, hold it upwards with your hands together and palms facing upwards, as you would an offering.

6. With your entire being as Benevolence, pour it into the Amulet. Do so until the Amulet is completely saturated with it, glowing and the feeling literally sweating out of the item. Declare loudly your intentions for the Amulet to become Benevolence itself.

7. When the feeling pours out of the Amulet like a thick fluid, dripping from your hands and streaming down your arms, hang it about your neck. Take a few moments more to cover it with your hands, the submissive cupping the dominant, and infuse this feeling into it for a bit longer. This last charge will "harden" the Emotion into the Charm, and the feeling will only lightly "sweat" out of the Amulet from this point on.

8. Stand, and thank the Spirits for their attendance. Offer them the gifts of thankfulness once again.

9. Part your Circle, and eat to conclude this exercise.

This Charm will invoke a need to assist others in all that surround you, and yourself. However, due to the fact that you will be wearing it constantly, it can become drained by neutralizing feelings of Malevolence you may encounter. If it begins to feel dry, or just to strengthen its ripple, take the time to repeat this exercise.

Exercise 3: The Rune of Warding

Runic symbols are dedicated to invoking a specific type of Emotional Energy wherever they are placed. A symbol will typically only be used to convey the same feeling, no matter how many times or in what places it is used, because all repetitions of the same symbol are ultimately linked together. For a Master craftsman of Runes, it is possible to change a plethora of repeated symbols to a new Emotional Energy. Use your Runes wisely.

1. Acquire the necessary means to craft your Rune. This may be simply pen and paper, but it can be as complex or simple as you like. For this exercise, you will be crafting a previously unused symbol, but one that you personally can recreate with ease.

2. Form a Magic Circle. Invite all Spirits to attend and take part in this Magical process, and offer them gifts.

3. Take a few moments to relax your body, breath, and mind.

4. For a Rune of Warding, you will wish to invoke the feeling of Terror. You must become this feeling; not a thing that stirs Terror in others, but the feeling of Terror itself.

5. Begin to craft your rune. With every stroke of pen, pencil, or brush, bond this feeling into the symbol itself. The power does not go into the ink or the paper, but into the shape of the Rune.

6. With the Rune completed, declare loudly that this is a Rune of Warding, by way of Terror.

7. Continue pouring the feeling into the symbol until it is completely saturated by it. The symbol itself should become as though it is entirely formed of the liquid of Terror.

8. When the symbol pulsates in waves of this feeling in both light, sound, and pressure, it is completed.

9. Destroy the medium upon which you crafted the symbol, but not the Rune itself.

10. Stand, and thank the Spirits for their attendance. Offer them the gifts you have brought once more.

11. Part your Circle, and eat.

The medium upon which you formed your Rune is destroyed because this frees the symbol from being bound to that medium. This allows you to draw the rune upon other items without it being bound solely to them. If you do not destroy the medium, it will be simply a charm, effective, but you will not have a Rune to work with. With the symbol freed from the medium, any other mediums upon which you place it can be destroyed, but the Rune will remain in that place until it has been dispelled. (As a side note, it is possible to draw a rune in the air with the finger and formed of Ether, and place it in close proximity to where this is performed.)

Exercise 4: The Seal of Protection

This exercise is a training in the technique of forming the Seal of Protection. Because the Pentagram is widely used for this same symbol across various Magic traditions, it is recommended that you also employ its usage with this technique. In Shamanism, the starting point of ascribing this symbol is not of importance; it is the essence of summoning the energy in which the ability lies. Do keep in mind, however, that the point of the star should be pointing skyward to symbolize aspiring to the One.

1. Begin by forming your Magic Circle. You will remain standing throughout this exercise.
2. Invite all Spirits to attend and take part in this ritual. Offer them those things that you feel will show your gratitude for their assistance. For

this ritual especially, this part is highly important, as the Spirits play a key role in assisting towards protection.

3. Loudly declare your intentions. State who, what, and why you wish protection for, as well as what it is you wish protection against.

4. Drawing in the air with Ether, form the shape of the Pentagram with the index finger of your dominant hand. You should see it burning a brilliant blue in the air when you inscribe it.

5. Once again, thank the Spirits for their attention and assistance, and invite them to partake of the gifts you have brought them.

6. End this exercise by parting your Circle and eating.

Runes and mystical symbols require a bit of finesse to craft, and with all other areas of Magic, the more you practice with specific techniques, the better your skill will become. Remember to solidly establish the precise feeling you wish to evoke with each symbol, and thank the Spirits each time you invoke a Rune.

The last area of Enchantment covered herein will be that of making the Doll and the Fetch. The Doll is a link between an item and a person, commonly referred to as the "Voodoo Doll." The Fetch is a Charm dedicated to seeking out and bringing to you goods, people, or situations. The next two exercises will cover the basics of the techniques utilized to form both of these.

Exercise 5: Forming the Doll

A Doll can be formed from many different materials, and must be created anew for each person you wish to link to it. Wax, clay, or bits of cloth are all that are needed to form your Doll. You should include within the Doll anything that links the person to it for you. When forming your Doll, it is not necessary for it to physically appear as the person you are link to it; it is the essence of their Soul that is attracted to the Doll that is necessary.

1. Assemble the materials of which you will form the Doll.
2. Form your Magic Circle, inviting the attendance and assistance of all Spirits and offering them gifts for their aid.
3. Seat yourself in the middle of the Circle and take a few moments to relax body, breath, and mind.
4. Declare your intentions for making the Doll, and of whom it will become.
5. Begin assembling your Doll. As you shape the material, it must become more and more of the person you are attracting with it. It is crucial that to you, there is no separation between the Doll and the person you are attracting to it.
6. When the Doll is completed, declare loudly that it is the person whom you were shaping it to be. Take a few moments to fiercely perceive it as such.
7. Stand, and thank the Spirits for their aid and attendance. Offer them your gifts of thankfulness once again.

8. Part your Circle and eat to conclude this exercise.

There are many ways a Doll can be used. Explore your options freely, and remember that you will reap what you sow.

Exercise 6: Shaping a Fetch

A Fetch is created in basically the same way as a Doll, but it is shaped in a way conducive to bringing to you what you wish. When you create a Fetch, you are taking aside a bit of yourself to form a "new" entity. When its goal is accomplished, this bit of you will return to you, but flavored in the way it was used.

1. Begin by acquiring items to form your Fetch with. Make certain that you include within it items that represent what you wish to attract; if it is the romantic interest of another, sweet smelling spices or similar things should be placed within; if it is something more malevolent, bits of nail, claw, or tooth.
2. Form your Magic Circle. Invite all Spirits to attend and take part in the process, and offer them gifts.
3. Seat yourself, and relax body, breath, and mind.
4. Declare loudly your intentions for making this Fetch.
5. As you assemble it, see the goal you intend for it in mind. Watch it bring it back to you.

6. When you complete the Fetch, thank it for its assistance and wish it luck.

7. Stand and thank the Spirits for their assistance, and once again offer the gifts you have set aside for them.

8. Part your Circle, then go out and bury the Fetch underneath a rock in a place that it will not be disturbed. When your goal has been met or it becomes evident that it is not to be, dig up your Fetch and burn it.

This concludes the section on Enchantment. Creativity and clarity of intention will allow you to achieve great deals of success in this area if you dedicate the time and effort for it. Always remember to use your Magic with care and consideration for all others, and it will be returned to you in a like manner.

Life Magic

The following section will be devoted to exercises in the practice of Life Magic. Life Magic is the art of using Ether and Life Fire to influence the well-being of another individual. Many of the techniques in this section require the sharing of your own energy with another, or directing Cosmic and Earth energies into them. With the highest degree of skill, it is possible to revive the dead with this type of Magic; however, the beginning goal should be only to influence the health of yourself and others into a more optimal state for longevity and the repelling of parasites.

For a beginner to practice this area of Magic, you must primarily be in a good state of health, and have a high store of energy which you can share. You must also be sensitive to both Ether and Life Fire as well as be able to direct the same. If you intend to find success in this branch of Magic practice, it is highly advisable to constantly practice Five Gates Breath, moderate your diet, and live a generally fit lifestyle.

Exercise 1: Aiding in a Swift Recovery

This first exercise in Life Magic will introduce you to pouring Ether and Life Fire into another individual in order to aid their recovery rate. Without a sufficient supply of Ether, and Ether converted to Life Fire, Material Manifestations cannot recover from damage. Consistent practice of this technique with the ailing while continuing to maintain your own health will generally lead one to the ability to instantly heal minor bruises and abrasions; with Mastery, it is possible to mend broken bones and other severe damages to the body.

1. Begin by making certain that your energy level is more than sufficient to maintain your current state of well-being.
2. Calm your breath, body, and mind.
3. Generate an Etheric Vortex underneath the wounded party with sufficient size to fuel you during this process.
4. Speak to the wounded individual with the desired result of relaxing them. Explain to them that although they may not feel anything during this process, slight electric tingling sensations are normal. This is the feeling of the energy infusing them.
5. As you speak to them, charge your hands with Ether. It is best to push gently on your exhales, and relax on your inhales until a siphon effect has been formed.
6. Move your palms over their body, feeling for disturbances with the charged hands. When a disturbance is felt, arc a gentle flow of Ether and Life Fire into them until the disturbance dissipates.
7. If you begin to feel tired or drained, stop immediately and regenerate your supply of Ether. If you are skilled at Five Gates Breath, this will not be a problem as you will find you are able to perform both the healing boost and the Breath at the same time.

8. Complete this technique by speaking positive statements of recovery to the individual. Explain to them that you could feel their energy system strengthening during the practice, even if they could not. It is also helpful to explain to them how to practice Deep Abdominal Breathing.

9. After the session, take an hour to wash out your energy system by pulling in Cosmic Ether from the head, and Earth Ether from the feet.

Exercise 2: Banishing Parasites

This technique will allow you to purge parasites from a host by burning them out with Ether. You must be able to view into the injured party's body and see the parasites, or at least feel their presence in order to direct the energy. The Ether used here should be a brilliant, freezing cold blue that burns as it strikes the target.

1. Begin by making certain that your energy level is sufficient enough to maintain your current state of well-being, and if possible, have an over-abundance of it.

2. Take a few moments to relax breath, body, and mind.

3. Form an Etheric Vortex underneath the infected individual.

4. Speak words of encouragement to the individual, and explain to them that they may or may not feel the tingling electrical sensations of the energy flowing through them.

5. With hands charged, feel over the person's body until the parasites are detected, all the while pouring Ether into them.

6. When the parasites are detected, focus intently upon them. With your Will, use the Ether to scour them from the victim's body.

7. If you are of sufficient energy level after burning out the parasites, continue to feed Ether into the wounded individual. Make positive statements about the improvement of their health.

8. When you feel you have completed the task or are becoming drained, stop and revitalize yourself. Take an hour after performing this to wash your energy system clean by pulling in Cosmic and Earth Ethers.

Do not force yourself to go beyond your energetic limits in any instance of using Life Magic. If your energy state drops below where it must be to maintain your own state of well-being, you will become ill. It is also important not to inhale the energies of the wounded party as you are performing the healing, for this will temporarily make you feel as they do. Always take the time before and after to cleanse and charge your system when working with Life Magic.

Exercise 3: Changing Flesh to Iron

This technique allows a practitioner to change their muscles and fascia from soft to an almost iron-like hardness by using a combination of deep breathing, isometric tension, and energy flow. With just a few years of practice of this technique, the body can be hardened to the point of resisting incredible blows that would be crushing to a normal individual. It also brings the body to a state that will repel most infections, and the dedicated practitioner should almost never become ill. As with any physical fitness program, you should consult your physician before beginning a new regimen.

1. Begin by dressing in loose, comfortable clothing and finding an area to practice in with good air circulation in which you will be undisturbed.

2. Relax your breath, body and mind. The breath is key to this exercise; it should be deep, relaxed, and smooth.

3. Do a bit of light stretching before the next step.

4. Stand with your back straight, knees slightly bent and shoulder length apart, and your hands out in front of you as though you are doing a push-up. Find total relaxation with this posture before proceeding.

5. When you exhale, tense all your muscles at once except for your head and facial muscles. This tension should be about half of the maximum tightness you are able to achieve with these muscles.

6. When you inhale, relax your body completely without losing the original posture. As you inhale, pull Ether into your entire body at once through your skin, and feel it permeate all the way down into the marrow of your bones.

7. Continue the process. In the beginning, you may only be able to complete ten breath cycles. Your goal is to reach 100. Work your way

up slowly; it is better to take your time, as you will find more success this way, than to attempt to rush and injure yourself in the process.

The key to this technique is being able to find and maintain the proper muscular tension as you exhale, and being able to find utter relaxation on the inhale. Develop this aspect of the exercise first before you attempt to pour Ether into yourself on your inhales. It is also helpful after completing the exercise to take a few moments to intensively practice Five Gates Breath, as this will more fully replenish your stores of Life Fire.

Exercise 4: Charging the Marrow

Consistent practice of this technique will enable your body to hold more vast stores of Ether and Life Fire than it was previously capable. For this reason, it has a long-standing reputation of increasing both longevity, clarity of perceptions, and the strength of Magic abilities. The practice consists of using a "flame" of Ether to purge the bones and marrow of grunge and an oily sludge that builds up within them over time.

This technique takes a vast amount of dedication and time to perform, and must be performed every single day until the entire bone structure is cleansed, and maintained daily after that point. The process of cleaning can take entire years, but it will enable you to literally view within your body and see every individual bone, organ, and tissue structure as you Will it. The daily progress will seem quite slow, but each miniscule bit of grunge cleared away is a massive improvement over what was. You may also note that you will need to "dust off" areas you have previously cleaned before progressing to the more caked on areas; this is normal accumulation that is picked up through our daily lives.

1. Begin this exercise by circulating your Aura and raising its energy level to the highest degree of which you are capable, without exhausting yourself. You will remain standing through this process, in a relaxed posture.

2. With your perception placed upon your fingertips, Will a heightened charge of Ether to be drawn into them. As you inhale, this Ether flares up within the bones themselves, burning brightly as a flame does with a draft. Start this at the very tips of the finger bones.

3. As you exhale, allow the flame to relax and push gently upon your Aura for circulation. This will transmute more Ether into your field, which you will direct into the next cleansing inhale.

4. Inhale again, with the purging Ether-flame burning a brilliant electric blue. It will move down the finger-bones as you Will the Ether into them; your Will should be placed only upon directing the Ether there. (side note: This Ether comes from your Aura around your hands, and not from the Life Fire within you.) When the flame lingers in a place, or seems difficult to push through an area, it is due to a blockage by the grunge and sludge found there. Increase the potency of the Ether-flame, and it will burn away. You may observe a "smoke" exuding from the area as this occurs.

5. Exhale. Turn your Aura with as much power as you are capable; see its brilliance, feel its force, and hear its song. Intensify this with each exhale, while keeping your breath deep and uniform.

6. Continue this cycle. As you progress, the bones themselves should come clearly into your perception, as with sight. Do not attempt to increase the rate of the cleaning and jump from area to area; it will move as it is to move.

Remember to practice this technique daily if you wish to actually complete it. The rewards are bountiful, but will not be listed herein. When you practice any technique, do not practice it for the sake of its rewards, but for the sake of the technique itself. With this perspective, you will find much greater success.

Necromancy

Necromancy is generally looked upon as "black" Magic, something evil and heretical. In truth, this branch of Life Magic deals with the resurrection of the dead, and the partial restoration of life to corpses themselves. This area of Life Magic can be routinely practiced by a Master, but it is possible for others to achieve results in the right circumstances.

Exercise 5: Ghouls

A ghoul is formed by pouring enough Life Fire into a corpse that it becomes revitalized. This Life Fire is not enough to completely repair the damage to the Material Manifestation, but sufficient enough to recall its Spirit and give it mobility as long as the Shaman continues to apply his own life in exchange. It is possible for the Shaman to die in the process of bringing another back in this manner.

1. Begin by making certain that your energy system is cleansed, your health is good, and your Emotions are stilled.

2. Forcefully rotate your Aura to the maximum of which you are capable, storing as much raw Ether within your belly as possible.

3. Make certain all clothing is removed from the corpse you will be reviving, and that it is not so deteriorated or mutilated as to be unable to achieve the task you will set before it.

4. Powerfully charge your hands. The Life Fire lies close to the skin in its Aura, so you must massage it into the flesh of the corpse. Pour your own life into the corpse as you massage it, through your hands, until you can see it beginning to circulate in their system.

5. This circulation is the sign of the Spirit's return to its Manifestation. Continue massaging when you see this, and with the exhales of your breathing, stream Ether into the mouth of the body you are working

with. The Spirit will be limitedly capable of transmuting Ether to Life Fire at this point, but it will lack the Ether given from his parents at the start of life which is used to draw in more of the same.

6. Continue working with the massage and transferring of Ether until the Ghoul is capable of moving about, and able to achieve the task you have set before him.

Extreme care must be taken when bringing up a Ghoul. It is possible for them to convince you to expend all of your Life Fire upon them, and at times, for the ghoul to grasp your energy and pull it all away from you. As long as the Ghoul is to remain, you must continue feeding your life into it. The next exercise will explain how to completely resurrect this Ghoul.

Exercise 6: Resurrection

1. Begin by following the procedure for a Ghoul.
2. Once the Spirit has returned, use your healing skills to repair the damage to the Material Manifestation that had previously ended its life.
3. Instruct the person on how to circulate their Aura, lending Ether to them as necessary.

It is possible to completely resurrect a person with one tremendous burst of Life Fire. As it takes a Master to perform this skill, it will not be detailed here. When you reach the point at which you will be able to perform this, you will know how to perform it.

If you attempt either one of these techniques and fail, do not be disheartened. Some Spirits will not return to their bodies. Also remember that what will be must be, for there is no other way. Some are not meant to return, and there are some things that we are not meant to do.

This concludes the section on Life Magic. Remember that it is of the utmost importance to first attend to your own health status before attempting to apply energy to heal another individual. If you are not in good overall health, you can seriously affect your own well-being by attempting to heal another. Also, if competent medical care by a trained physician is available, allow them to do their work before you do yours. Complementing the work of a doctor with Magic is always a much better route than attempting to assume the role of healer and failing where modern medical treatment would have been effective.

The Perceptive Arts

The Perceptive Arts is the branch of Magic techniques that allows you to gather information by means not accessible to the five senses. Prophetic dreams and visions, bone-casting, Tarot, crystal-gazing, reading tea leaves, and accessing knowledge of the Universal Consciousness are all techniques of the Perceptive Arts. These techniques fall into one of the categories of Divination, Scrying, or Clairvoyance. The next few exercises will cover practices in each of these areas.

Divination

Divination is the art of reading omens and portents. This art relies heavily upon the ability of the Shaman to understand the way currents of Emotional Energy affect the entire world, and by seeing the way they are now moving, to be able to accurately predict the way events will occur. Divining future events is similar to forecasting the way a lily pad will move based on the way the ripples of pond water strike the shoreline. Success in Divination takes practice and observation. Keep in mind as well that Divination is not fortune-telling; unseen motions of energy can and will affect possible outcomes. The only certain outcome for the future is change itself.

<u>Tarot</u>

One of the most well-known methods of Divination is Tarot. This mode employs a deck of 78 cards, each representing different degrees of Emotion and the most likely changes to occur as a result of the force from an Emotion. The Tarot deck is divided into two parts: the Major Arcana, and the Minor Arcana. For the purposes of this book, the Minor Arcana will not be discussed.

The Major Arcana consists of 22 cards which represent Emotional forces of change and the Material forces of change which are motivated in conjunction with these. They are numbered from 0-21 and each contains symbolism pertaining to the various meanings of each card as well as being an archetype for the pathway to Awakening and True Sight of the One. It should be noted that card meanings are not concrete, they are and should remain extremely flexible with the final determination of card meaning being left up to the person performing the reading.

Card 0 is **The Fool**. This archetype represents the beginning of the journey, the opening point of awareness. At this level of the journey, the Seeker is still perceiving things the way he expects them to be. This card symbolizes: the beginning of a journey; failure to understand details; recklessness; delusion; euphoria or excitement; and Hubris. When inverted, it symbolizes: slothfulness; Apathy; hesitancy; lack of informed judgment leading to poor choices; and poor vision of opportunity.

Card 1 is **The Magician**. This archetype represents the first leg of the journey, when the Awareness of the Fool has been kindled and he begins to seek understanding. This card symbolizes: Coordination; exercised Will; Creative genius; Treachery; the drive to Mastery; and Confidence. Inverted meanings are: lack of creative power; Will harnessed for destructive ends; loss or lack of confidence; and unnecessary delay.

Card 2 is **The Wise Woman**. This archetype represents the transition into understanding by experience, and the wisdom gained from experience. The Magician through practice has begun to see, and has gained understanding from this new sight. This card symbolizes: Wisdom; compassion; the understanding of effects; instruction; learning; and separation of Awareness from the influence of Emotion. Inverted meanings are: lack of understanding; Awareness and perception influenced by Emotion; the failure to learn by experience; and the inability to share in the feelings of others.

Card 3 is **The Empress**. This archetype represents the union of understanding and practice, causing fertility in action. By the skill of the Magician and the understanding of the Wise Woman, the Fool becomes able to perceive how and why the forces of change move, and thus is able to harness them to beneficial ends. This card symbolizes: change by acceptance; Intuitive understanding; fertility; the ability to lead by example; motivation; decisions founded on understanding of the facts at hand; and a close female kin. Inverted meanings are: Infertility of action; material loss; misguidance; lack of motivation; vanity; and stunted progress.

Card 4 is **The Emperor**. This archetype represents the progression from Acceptance into Willful change of those things which have been understood and accepted. This card symbolizes: Authority; Material Wealth; a close male kin; a Patriarch; the desire to dominate all; a capable and worthy person to exercise authority; and the willingness to heed the advice of others. Inverted means are: Overwhelming by Emotion; Weakness; inability to mature; intentional ignorance; and indecisive action.

Card 5 is **The Old Man**. This archetype represents the progression into a uniform routine, and a loss of the essence of why the journey was begun. This card symbolizes: Inability to adapt to new situations; Gentility; humility; a spiritually knowledgeable individual; the importance of history; and the loss of sight due to one's own ideas. Inverted meanings are: Fragility; loss of sensitivity to effects; Vulnerability; and repeating errors that are known to be errors.

Card 6 is **The Lovers**. This archetype represents releasing the way you perceive in order to attain True Sight, and the discarding of the woody traditions for the suppleness of change. This card symbolizes: the realization of beauty in the mundane; perfection by integration; gaining insight from lessons of situation; the overcoming of trials; Affection, and blindness by the same; the release of self; the ability to feel Emotion without being overcome by it; and unification. Inverted meanings are: failure to acknowledge lessons; inability to perceive beauty and truth; loss of affection; destroyed unity; lack of dedication; and irresponsibility.

Card 7 is **The Chariot**. This archetype represents the journey into change, and the inner battle we must wage with ourselves to come to accept constant change. This card symbolizes: triumph over adversity; the need to harness Emotion; a swift journey into the unknown; greatness achieved by maintaining control over action and Emotion; and the necessity of details. Inverted meanings are: inability to harness Emotion; inability to utilize True Sight; to have a goal of import slip from the grasp; and failure.

Card 8 is Justice. This archetype represents the balance of opposing forces and the realization that all things seek a return to simplicity. This card symbolizes: Equality; Justice; Righteousness in all things; the ability to avoid destructive temptations;

consideration; and honorable intentions. Inverted meanings are: Injustice; immorality as defined by the self; biased perception; unfairness; and non-acceptance.

Card 9 is **The Hermit**. This archetype represents the recession into self in order to attain understanding. This card symbolizes: self-enlightenment; good advice; patience; the denial of self; possession of secrets; knowledge for the sake of knowledge; and withdrawal. Inverted meanings are: lack of patience; taking premature actions; faulty advice; failure to act; and isolation from reality.

Card 10 is **The Wheel of Fortune**. This archetype represents insight of Fate and the knowledge to carve Destiny, which can only be achieved by attaining understanding of the self. This card symbolizes: Material wealth; disruptive change; Destiny; approaching outcome; and an unexpected turn of events. Inverted meanings are: loss of material wealth; ill-favored events; meddling of affairs by others; and failure.

Card 11 is **Force**. This archetype represents the balance that comes from being able to walk within the Material and Spiritual worlds simultaneously. This card symbolizes: Attainment in the face of peril; control of Destiny; Passion; talent; Strength to overcome all obstacles; and self-confidence. Inverted meanings are: failure to overcome obstacles; illness; weakness; petty retaliation; indifference to abuse; and the loss of Will.

Card 12 is **The Hanged Man**. This archetype represents sacrificing the uplifting of self for the good of All. This card symbolizes: self-sacrifice; change; apathy; a goal which cannot be reached; surrender; and lack of appreciation. Inverted meanings are: useless sacrifice; inability to sacrifice self; consumption of the self; and false prophecy.

Card 13 is **Death**. This archetype represents the transformation of the self, when it is set aside for the good of All. This card symbolizes: change; loss of material wealth; the death of old ways; and illness or physical death. Inverted meanings are: lack of change; slow changes; and the avoidance of an ill favored event.

Card 14 is **Temperance**. This archetype represents the alignment of the self with the All, and harmonious accord between the two. This card symbolizes: patience; moderation; fusion; accomplishment by self-control; and accommodation. Inverted meanings are: conflict; discord; impatience; hostility; lack of empathy with others; and loss of self-control.

Card 15 is **The Devil**. This archetype represents the desire to uplift the self at the expense of the All. This card symbolizes: Imprisonment; mischievous deeds; bad advice; malice; spite; self-destruction; temptation to do evil; destructive magic; lack of empathy with others; and only being humored by another's injury. Inverted meanings are: freedom from bonds; the advancement of True Sight; Divorce; and compassion of others.

Card 16 is **The Falling Tower**. This archetype represents the end effect of uplifting the self at the expense of the All; the effort ends in futility. This card symbolizes: broken foundations; loss of old beliefs; loss of friends; destruction of trust; destructive change; and misery. Inverted meanings are: adhering to the old and rejecting the new; inability to make beneficial change; imprisonment; and unhappiness.

Card 17 is **The Star**. This archetype represents the realization that occurs when it is realized that uplifting the self is futile. This card symbolizes: Hope; love; happiness brought about by desire and work; and satisfaction. Inverted meanings are:

disappointment; stubbornness; lack of balance; loss of hope; unfulfilled hopes; and pessimism.

Card 18 is **The Moon**. This archetype represents the understanding of motives brought about by True Sight. This card symbolizes: deception; bad influences; false friends; slander; unknown enemies; ulterior motives; and failure to avoid dangers. Inverted meanings are: recognition of deception; enemies revealed; overcoming destructive temptations; and gain at another's expense.

Card 19 is **The Sun**. This archetype represents the satisfaction gained from beneficial changes made at the expense of hard work. This card symbolizes: satisfaction; joy; contentment; warmth; sincerity; a new friendship; and pleasure from simplicity. Inverted meanings are: Delay of resolution; unhappiness; lack of friendships; and a lost partnership.

Card 20 is **Judgment**. This archetype represents the understanding by experience of how effects shape existence. This card symbolizes: the conclusion of a conflict; the need to forgive, both oneself and others; a desire for immortality; and the reward of effort. Inverted meanings are: failure to forgive oneself or others; a situation where one is taking unfair advantage of another; the failure to face reality; procrastination; and attempting to delay the inevitable.

Card 21 is **The World**. This archetype represents the final stage in Awakening, where true understanding of the All is attained. This card symbolizes: Completion; fulfillment; success through effort; immortality; admiration; and material wealth. Inverted meanings are: failing to finish a task; the inability to recognize within oneself what would be considered flaws, or to correct the same; greed; and the inability to perceive things as they truly are.

To initiate a reading, begin by organizing the Major Arcana into order from 0-21, with the Fool on the top of the deck. Instruct the person for whom you will be reading to construct their question in the following format, without telling you what the question is: "What will be the outcome of (certain situation) if I continue to do as I am now doing?" After they acknowledge that the question has been formed, hand them the stack of cards and instruct them to allow their question to soak into the cards from their hands like an electric blue liquid, with the cards absorbing it as a sponge would water. Tell them to shuffle the cards as they do this, any way they choose, with attention being placed upon the question soaking into the cards rather than the way they shuffle. The shuffling should stop when they feel that the cards can absorb no more of the question.

When the shuffling is complete, take the cards from the person being read. Turn the deck around so that you are holding it the same way the person who shuffled it was. Lay down the first seven cards in a row. These seven cards will determine the reading.

The first card laid down represents minor outside forces affecting the situation. The second represents major outside forces affecting the situation. The third card gives advice in handling these outside influences.

The fourth card represents the conscious desire of the person for whom the reading is being given in regards to the situation. The fifth card represents unconscious desires of the person regarding the situation. The sixth card gives advice in reference to the state of mind approaching the situation.

The seventh card represents the final outcome of this situation, if all things are to remain as they are. The true purpose of this card is not to predict the future, but to give the person a chance to change the destination that is already being progressed towards. This card should be taken as advice more than as a prediction of future events. After this card has been turned, it is up to the person for whom the reading was done to decide whether or not they feel comfortable in sharing the question. It is not required that they do so, and this should be explained to them; although knowing the question can sometimes help the reader to define the cards more thoroughly.

The purpose of divining by means of Tarot is to give you a chance to see where things are going now and to change it. Make certain that this idea is expressed clearly to anyone for whom you are performing a reading. Also be certain explain to them that this is not a method of seeing into the future with certainty; once the future is known, it can be changed and is therefore no longer set.

Scrying

Scrying is a technique in which the Shaman peers into an object in order to set his mind aside and view into the present. This method differs from Divination in that the practitioner relies upon their connection to the Universal Consciousness to directly gain the knowledge that is being sought. It is difficult to explain exactly how to enter into the receptive state, so practice must be maintained until you understand the method that is best for you. The method for Scrying contained herein will be for gazing into smoke.

1. Begin by preparing your pipe and smoking materials. Some will find Nicotiana Rustica to be efficient for practice, though some may prefer to Scry by means of Cannabis Sativa or Papaver Somniferum preparations.

2. Seat yourself in a comfortable place, relatively devoid of wind. Have the question in mind, and displace all distractive thoughts.

3. Begin lighting your pipe. You will wish to form a thick bank of smoke to peer into.

4. As the smoke bank forms, peer into it, and allow your question to settle into the smoke bank. Relax your consciousness, so that your awareness expands.

5. You will find that as soon as your mind relaxes and you have freed the question, visions or voices will be found within the cloud, by your awareness. Travel through these until your answer is found.

6. When completed, thank the plant from which your smoking material was obtained.

The answer you find for the question may not be quite what you expect it to be. There are times when a direct answer is not right for the occasion; in these cases, advice for proceeding or another question itself may be presented to you. If another individual offers you information while Scrying, decline their assistance respectfully. Inform that entity that the information you seek must be found by you, and wish them safety and peace in their parting.

There are many variations to this technique. It can be performed by gazing deeply into practically any item. Success depends upon the practitioner's ability to detach so that awareness can expand beyond its normal coverage.

<u>Clairvoyance</u>

Clairvoyance is the ability to perceive things not presently discernable by the five senses. This is possible for one who is sensitive to Ether, as the movement of any small amount affects the movement of all. For this reason, the best training for this technique relies in Circulating the Aura and Five Gates Breath. You must be able to expand your awareness across the Ether to determine whatever it is you seek. This ability cannot be taught or adequately explained. It is often something simply stumbled upon in practice. The key is to literally become the moment; when you are the moment, all things are known.

This concludes the section on the Perceptive Arts. It is highly advisable for you to train in the techniques you wish to employ with skill on a regular basis. It should also be known that this is in no way a complete listing of techniques for perception; there are many more guides and techniques than are listed here. Keep in mind that developing a keen sense of perception will also enable you to rediscover techniques that have been lost or obscure.

Spiritism

Spiritism is the art of communicating direct understanding to other Spirits, and having direct understanding communicated to you. For humans, one of the unfortunate downfalls of this practice is a common tendency to translate the communication to ourselves into words to be processed by the forefront of our mind and analyzed. Rarely do we accept the message consciously as it is presented to us. This type of communication is not Telepathy, for telepathy is a broadcast of information from one entity to another; this type of information is the direct exchange of experience by union of the two Spirits. Contained within this section will be exercises in Telepathy with plants and animals, and for Mediumship and Channeling of Spirits.

Exercise 1: Plant Telepathy

1. Begin this exercise by selecting a plant that you cultivate or encounter on a regular basis, that you feel would be generally amiable to your presence.

2. Seat yourself comfortably beside the plant, where you will be facing it. Begin relaxing body, breath, and mind.

3. When you feel completely relaxed and free of distractive thoughts, greet the plant. If you speak out loud, use soft words, but project well-formed vocalized thought at the plant as you speak. The thoughts from your

head should boom with a strong voice, but the mental voice should not be yelling or screaming.

4. Take the time to wait for a response from the plant. Keep your thoughts silenced, or you will not be able to hear. Plants tend to project very softly when they communicate; it is your duty to listen to the plant, not the plant's duty to overwhelm your other thoughts so the message gets across.

5. Hold a conversation with the plant as you would with any other person, taking the same polite considerations. Make sure you pause and give the plant plenty of time to speak with you. While not being shy, they are very much reserved unless you happen upon one that's not amiable to you.

6. When the conversation is completed, thank the plant for the opportunity to converse, and offer it a farewell as you would with any friend.

This exercise can be practiced with nearly any plant, once you grasp the technique for listening. Continue speaking with the same plant day after day; if you are working with those you cultivate, you will find that a good time to chat will be while you are tending to them.

Exercise 2: Animal Telepathy

1. Begin this exercise by introducing yourself to an animal. It does not matter if it is wild or domesticated, but it is best to practice this with an animal that is not considered to be a pet.

2. Introduce yourself to the animal. Speak with it the same way you would with anyone that you greatly respect. Use the same mental silence to hear responses as you do when conversing with plants.

3. The approach of animals in conversation varies wildly by the animal and by the way the animal feels about you. If it's afraid of you, it will be reflected by the way it communicates to you. Telling it not to worry alone will not assuage its fears; you have to use body language. This is due to the feral nature of the animal, and it can be overcome with time if you are communicating repeatedly with the same individual.

4. When you are finished conversing with the animal, thank it for the chat and offer a friendly farewell.

It sometimes helps to offer food to the animal you are communicating with. This puts them physically at ease, and helps to free their mind from stress so they are better able to speak with you. Take care whenever feeding any wild animal; sometimes it is most wise to simply converse from a safe distance and keep the reference for food far away from yourself.

Exercise 3: Mediumship

1. Begin by having a specific Spirit selected with whom you will communicate.
2. Prepare your work area. It should be free of distractions and most energetic influences. If any will be present during the Mediumship, instruct them to remain quiet and relaxed.
3. Seat yourself comfortably and relax body, breath, and mind. At the point of complete relaxation, reach out with your feelings and touch the Spirit with whom you will communicate.
4. At the point of communication, you must release all bonds to the Material Plane and your current persona so that you will be able to unify with the Spirit in mind.
5. Once the transference has occurred, take a few moments to settle yourself and remember who you are on this Material Plane. If you were playing Medium for another individual who is unable to perform this, communicate the message to them at this time.

When you practice this exercise, it is a good idea to keep a journal of who you are attempting to reach, what the results were, how long it took, and how you felt afterwards.

This will allow you to better understand your personal technique for Mediumship and allow you to streamline your exercise and practice.

Exercise 4: Channeling

1. Arrange for some method of recording this exercise, as you will most probably not remember completely all the details.

2. Begin as above, by relaxing yourself and reaching out to the Spirit you wish to communicate with.

3. Allow the Spirit to share your Material Manifestation with you, so that the two of you become blended together with neither overcoming the other.

4. Allow those present, if any, to ask questions for the Spirit in question to respond to.

5. When completed and the Spirit takes leave, take a few moments to center yourself and remember who you are and what your place is on this Material Plane.

6. Eat a bit of food, and drink a bit of water.

7. Review the recording and set it aside for later evaluation.

When Channeling, possession is never a threat. It is never a threat because no entity can control you directly from your mind. Situations of possession and control always arise through either leading the victim's responses, or by conditioning the victim to respond in a manner of subservience. Neither of this will occur when your Spirit is mixed with that of another for the purposes of communication.

This concludes the section on Spiritism. Please understand that these techniques listed here are not all inclusive or the only means to achieve these results. Practice and experiment, and your understanding will increase with experience.

Limitless Possibilities

With understanding, the possibilities for working magic and the effects achieved thereby are completely limitless. It is highly important for your progression that you develop techniques on your own by experimentation. Always keep in mind that the structure and the tools do not contain the magic; it is you that contains the Will. Structure and tools are simply there to enable you a greater ability to focus. Work to overcome these, so that the magic is pure and spontaneous transformation of energy and forces.

The responsibility for your existence lies solely with you. It's not what happens to you, it's what you do. This is true for all things. For instance, when it begins to rain and you get wet, is it what happens to you, or are you allowing yourself to be rained upon? If you are dissatisfied with your situation, remember that only you have the power to remain in it, and the power to change it. Even passivity is an active state of doing.

Always show respect for others around you. We are all One. Dedicate this approach to all of your relationships, and remember that preservation of self and offspring is the prime right of Material Manifestations. Through cooperation with and realization that we are one with our environment, this prime right can be most readily achieved.

It is imprudent to attempt to use magical means for every circumstance. Some things are best achieved by more material means. If you need sustenance, work for it. Don't throw energy around and expect to have it fall out of the sky. Though this is most certainly possible, it is a waste of valuable resources. There is always an equal exchange when we work magic.

It is my hope that you found this guide helpful in your progress. I cannot hand the experience or the understanding of experience to you. The path is illuminated. Walk it with care, and remember that the act of walking is not the journey itself.

Bibliography

Abadie, M.J. *Your Psychic Potential.* Adams Media, 1995.

Andrews, Shirley. *Lemuria and Atlantis: Studying the Past to Survive the Future.* Llewellyn, 2004.

Belanger, Michelle. *The Psychic Vampire Codex.* Weiser, 2004.

Conway, D.J. *By Oak, Ash, & Thorn: Modern Celtic Shamanism.* Llewellyn, 1995.

Cunningham, Scott. *Cunningham's Encyclopedia of Crystal, Gem & Metal Magic.* Llewellyn, 1988.

De Angeles, Ly. *Witchcraft: Theory and Practice.* Llewellyn, 2000.

Dong, Paul, and Raffill, Thomas E. *China's Super Psychics.* Marlowe & Company, 1997.

Fetrow, Charles W. and Avila, Juan R. *The Complete Guide to Herbal Medicines.* Pocket Books, 2000.

Gerber, Richard, M.D. *A Practical Guide to Vibrational Medicine: Energy Healing and Spiritual Transformation.* Harper Collins, 2000.

Gottlieb, Adam. *Psilocybin Production.* Ronin, 1997.

Govinda, Lama Anagarika. *Foundations of Tibetan Mysticism.* Weiser, 1969.

Kraig, Donald Michael. *Modern Magick: Eleven Lessons in the High Magickal Arts, Second Edition.* Llewellyn, 1998.

Kravette, Steve. *Complete Meditation.* Whitford Press, 1982.

Lee, Bruce, edited by Little, John. *Jeet Kune Do: Bruce Lee's Commentaries on the Martial Way, Volume Three.* Tuttle Publishing, 1997.

Liao, Waysun, translated and with commentary by. *T'ai Chi Classics.* Shambhala, 1990.

Lu, K'uan Yu. *Taoist Yoga.* Weiser, 1973.

Osho. *The Book of Secrets.* St. Martin's Griffin, 1974.

Oss, O.T., and Oeric, O.N. *Psilocybin: The Magic Mushroom Grower's Guide.* Quick American, 1991.

Ott, Jonathan. *Ayahuasca Analogues.* Natural Products, 1994.

Panchadasi, Swami. *Clairvoyance and Occult Powers.* Yogi Publication Society, 1916.

Pinchbeck, Daniel. *Breaking Open the Head.* Broadway Books, 2002.

Reid, Daniel. *A Complete Guide to Chi-Gung: Harnessing the Power of the Universe.* Simon & Schuster, 1998.

Sanders, Pete A., Jr. *You Are Psychic! The Free Soul Method.* Fireside, 1989.

Shum, Leung. *The Secrets of Eagle Claw Kung Fu: Ying Jow Pai.* Tuttle, 2001.

Slate, Joe H., Ph.D. *Psychic Vampires: Protection From Energy Predators and Parasites.* Llewellyn, 2002.

Stamets, Paul. *Psilocybin Mushrooms of the World: An Identification Guide.* Ten Speed Press, 1996.

Tyson, Donald. *Scrying for Beginners: Tapping into the Supersensory Powers of Your Subconscious.* Llewellyn, 1997.

Wong, Kiew Kit. *The Complete Book of Tai Chi Chuan.* Element Books, 1996.

Yang, Jwing-Ming, Dr. The Essence of Shaolin White Crane. YMAA, 1996.

Internet Resources

Http://mulga.yage.net

Http://www.aros.net/~lambo/

Http://www.cocomama.com

Http://www.elftrance.com

Http://www.entheology.org

Http://www.erowid.org

Http://www.iboga.com

Http://www.pearyhenson.org/trichocereus/

Http://www.sagewisdom.org

Http://www.shroomery.com

Http://www.usna.usda.gov

Http://www.xs4all.nl/~knehnav/

Index

Acupuncture *pp. 59*

Alchemy *pp. 70*

Altered States *pp. 77*

Ascetics *pp. 51*

Aura *pp. 54,69*

Auric Tendrils *pp. 63, 177*

Awakening *pp. 34*

Awareness *pp. 31,38*

Ayahuasca *pp. 163*

Bermuda Triangle *pp. 67*

Billiard Ball *pp. 172*

Cannabis Sativa *pp. 215*

Carnal *pp. 34, 78*

Carpophore *pp. 133*

Caveman *pp. 157*

Channeling *pp. 221-222*

Charm *pp. 184*

Clairvoyance *pp. 216*

Cloak of Shadows *pp. 153-154, 157*

Communion *pp. 80, 91-93*

Conjuring *pp. 41*

Corpse *pp. 202*

Dead Zones *pp. 66*

Delusions *pp. 77-78*

Devil's Triangle *pp. 67*

Doppelganger *pp. 161*

Earth Aura *pp. 51, 65*

Ego *pp. 76*

Elemental Magic *pp. 41*

Elemental States *pp. 166*

Emotional Energies *pp. 17, 21, 26*

Emotional Empathics *pp. 42*

Emotional Energy Centers *pp. 55*

Emotional Temper *pp. 58-59*

Emotional Vibration *pp. 11*

Empathy *pp. 175*

Enchantment *pp. 42*

Enlightened Ones *pp. 12*

Enlightenment *pp. 20*

Ether *pp. 56, 60, 64, 68, 72, 85*

Evil *pp. 24-25*

Experimentation *pp. 223*

Fascia *pp. 198*

Fetch *pp. 191, 193-194*

Flesh *pp. 79*

Five Gates Breath *pp. 61, 149, 195*

Foci *pp. 44*

Follow the Breath *pp. 31, 43, 149*

Fortune-telling *pp. 206*

Ghoul *pp. 203-204*

Good *pp. 24-25*

Great Spirit *pp. 13*

Guidelines for Magic *pp. 39*

Hallucinations *pp. 77-78*

Holy Days *pp. 80-83*

Kill *pp. 25*

Ley Line *pp. 66*

Life Fire *pp. 15, 17, 59, 69, 195*

Life Magic *pp. 42*

Love *pp. 35*

Lust *pp. 176*

Lycanthropy *pp. 163-165*

Magic Circle *pp. 50-51*

Magic Effects *pp. 85, 89, 98*

Magic Sand *pp. 52*

Magical Empowerment *pp. 98-99*

Marrow *pp. 200*

Material Consciousness *pp. 12*

Material Plane *pp. 10, 12*

Meditation *pp. 29, 33, 78*

Mediumship *pp. 220-221*

Mycelia *pp. 131*

Necromancy *pp. 202*

Offspring *pp. 25*

Omens *pp. 206*

Oracle *pp. 96-97*

Original Motion *pp. 10, 16*

Papaver Somniferum *pp. 215*

Path of the Shaman *pp. 148*

Pendulum *pp. 171*

Perceptive Arts *pp. 42*

Plant Spirits *pp. 79, 88*

Prayer Beads *pp. 185-186*

Primal Desire *pp. 12*

Qigong *pp. 59*

Radio Frequency *pp. 169*

Reality *pp. 21*

Resurrection *pp. 204*

Ritual *pp. 74-76*

Rune *pp. 184*

Sacred Teacher Plants *pp. 78-79, 80, 88, 89, 145*

San Pedro *pp. 163*

Seduce *pp. 178*

Sex *pp. 23*

Shaman *pp. 27*

Shroud, the *pp. 14, 21, 40, 50*

Spell *pp. 73-74, 76*

Spiritism *pp. 43*

Spore Print *pp. 133*

Substrate *pp. 130-131*

Stone *pp. 84*

Tarot *pp. 207-214*

Telepathy *pp. 217*

Terrarium *pp. 131-132*

Third-Eye *pp. 33, 69*

Three Vibrations *pp. 10-11, 14*

Transmuting *pp. 84*

Ultimate, the *pp. 10*

Universal Consciousness *pp. 10-11, 13, 206, 214*

Unseen Ones *pp. 67*

Vampire *pp. 63*

Vision Quest *pp. 94-95*

Visualize *pp. 38*

Vortex *pp. 57, 70*

Watchers *pp. 94-95*

Will *pp. 27-28, 38, 74, 151*

Witch *pp. 73*

Wizard *pp. 73*

Wyrms *pp. 53, 58, 179-183*

Voodoo Doll *pp. 191*

Yin-Yang *pp. 13*

Printed in Great Britain
by Amazon